Peace Beyond the Tears:

Hope After Sexual Betrayal

by Tina Harris

featuring the
Counselor's Corner
with Diane Roberts

Foreword by Steven Arterburn

Peace Beyond the Tears:

Hope After Sexual Betrayal
by Tina Harris

Counselor's Corner with Diane Roberts

ISBN 978-0-9896598-7-1

Linda Dodge, Editor

Published by
Pure Desire Ministries International
Gresham, Oregon
www.puredesire.org
March 2014

Peace Beyond the Tears
Contents

Acknowledgements

Tim, you are my best friend and hero. Thank you for encouraging me throughout the writing of this book and for doing the hard work necessary to heal.

To my six amazing daughters: I love you so much! I am proud of each one of you.

Thank you . . .

. . . Doug Barnes, for being my link to reality.

. . . Larry Sonnenburg for challenging me to write this book!

. . . Alisa Keeton and all my friends at Revelation Wellness who taught me through the Grand Canyon experience that God is the great "I AM."

I am grateful to New Life Ministries and Pure Desire Ministries for being there to show us the way.

Thank you Diane Roberts for believing in me and making my dream for this book a reality, and to Linda Dodge for her wonderful editing and formatting.

Thank you, God, for always being there and for turning my mourning into dancing (Psalm 30:11).

God bless you all!

Tina

| Peace Beyond the Tears

Foreword

I have had the good fortune of knowing Tina and Tim for many of the years they have worked together through problems of connection, sexual integrity, and the ups and downs of recovery. I was just with them today and they are in a good place. As you read on, you will find that was not always the case, especially for Tina, who began her journey when women in her situation we being demeaned and dismissed rather than seen, heard, understood, and helped.

For years, when a couple went through a problem with sexual integrity, sexual addiction treatment was all about the offending male and his need to identify, treat, and stop what he had been doing to sever the relationship. It was all about what it would take for a man to be able to give up his sexual acting out, such as looking at dirty pictures or visiting massage parlors, or paying for prostitutes. This was important and mandatory for recovery, but it fell way too short of what was needed to help a sex addict.

In our Every Man's Battle treatment program, I think we were much more focused in this direction in the beginning. Now we know that effective treatment must identify and address the destructive schemes and secretive behavior patterns that demeaned the wife. At New Life and Women In The Battle, we began taking a deeper look into what was needed for the spouse, in large part because of Tina's story, her encouragement to us to make some changes, and her persevering spirit.

When we started working with Tina on this book several years ago, she was not ready to write it. She humbly waited until she was ready, and now she has a book with a story that will change lives.

Tina recently spoke again to all of our men going through Every Man's Battle. I read their comments about her. Some cried for their wives for the first time. Some considered their wife's pain for the first time. Others saw a courageous woman who wanted to help some men be healing to their wives.

This is a powerful story from a powerful woman, and I hope you are inspired to heal deeper, walk taller, and connect more authentically with others than ever before.

If you have been hurt by a man and feel there is no hope for your future. I believe this book, this story, is going to change your mind.

Stephen Arterburn
Author of *Every Man's Battle*
Host of New Life Live

Preface

Dear Friend,

Several years ago my world turned upside down with the new knowledge of my husband's sexual sin. All I wanted was for someone to come beside me and tell me it was going to be alright, someone to tell me what came next and that I was not alone. I needed a friend who would not judge, give me unsolicited advice, or condemn my husband. I desperately needed someone to tell me what life could look like on the other side, and that there was, in fact, an "other" side. But I could find no one. I was alone and scared, afraid of my own feelings and afraid of what lay ahead.

Now that my journey has moved to a place of peace beyond the tears, I have set out to be that friend to as many people as possible. I am telling my story in an effort to be authentic, to let you know there is hope, and there is an "other" side. You are NOT alone and your feelings are valid. Most of all, I hope to show you that our awesome God is right beside you, even if you don't feel His presence right now.

Next fall I am planning to hike twenty-three miles in thirteen hours from one rim of the Grand Canyon to the other. This is one of the many endeavors that God has put in front of me these past few years—adventures I never would have attempted before I knew of Tim's addiction. Because of the new relationship that I have with God and because of the trust I have in Him, I know that I can accomplish anything with God on my side.

Years ago if you had asked me about myself, I probably would have said something about being a wife, a mother, a Sunday School teacher. But now when I picture my life, I see open spaces and no walls. If I were to draw you a visual of my life now, I would draw myself on the other side of the Grand Canyon with my arms up to the sky, tears of joy streaming down my face as I praise the God who sees me and loves me unconditionally! I can only imagine what it is going to feel like to hike from one side of the Grand Canyon to the other, to look around at how far I have come and the deep chasm that now separates me from my past. I imagine I will be apprehensive as we hike down, not knowing what to expect; then I think I might be a bit overwhelmed as we start to climb back up, wondering if I will be able to make it all the way up. As we get closer to the top, I will start to feel excitement when at last the rim is visible and we see people cheering us on to completion.

I pray that no matter where you are on your journey back to the top that you have people around you, cheering you on. I pray that you know God is right beside you, walking each and every step with you, that you know you are not alone on this journey, and that many people you have never met are praying for you. And I pray that you, too, will be able to make it to the other side, praising God and knowing how much He loves you.

You are in my heart and prayers, dear friend. May God bless you on your journey! See you at the top!

Counselor's Corner

Revelation 12 tells us about the power of sharing our testimonies. Tina's story will give you ability to see hope in the midst of your pain. Within the ***Counselor's Corner*** we want to add definition to sexual addiction and broaden your understanding of how your husband's bondage has impacted you. Our hope is that you will use the tools and helps we include to process the horrendous byproduct of pain, fear, and anger that you as the spouse are experiencing.

In *Peace Beyond the Tears,* Tina beautifully walks out Paul's admonition in 2 Corinthians 1:3-4:

Blessed be the God and Father of our Lord Jesus Christ, the Father of mercies and God of all comfort, who comforts us in our tribulation, that we may be able to comfort those who are in any trouble with the comfort with which we ourselves are comforted by God.

Peace Beyond the Tears

Introduction

Early one morning, shortly after Tim attended the Every Man's Battle workshop, I was sitting on the couch trying to read my Bible. I couldn't concentrate so I decided to write down my feelings in my journal. The result was the story of a young doll named Tina who sat around waiting for her husband to pay her some attention and to love her.

Doll Story: A Fictional Tale

There was once a doll maker who made beautiful dolls. Dolls for young men to adore, love, and with whom to share their lives. This doll maker crafted each doll with the greatest of care. He would pick the finest fabrics for the clothes and polish the dolls until they shined. He would give them the soft, bright hair and would put a sparkle in their eyes. And when he was almost finished, he would put a heart in them that desired complete oneness, affection, and attention from the young man who would purchase her.

One such doll named Tina had a rough start. Her paint was never quite right, her clothes never quite fit, and her eyes just didn't twinkle. People would come in to watch the doll maker and say, "She's not right." But the doll maker assured Tina that some day she would be wanted. One day some young man would love her, desire her, and make her feel like she mattered. So Tina waited and dreamed of the day she would be cherished.

One day a young man came and took Tina down from the shelf. He played with her for a while and promised her happiness. But he dropped her and chipped her, which made her feel worthless. Then he put her back on the shelf and told the doll maker that she was bad and broken.

Tina was heartbroken, but not for long. Very soon afterwards a young man named Tim walked into the doll shop and purchased Tina, chips and all. He promised her love and passion. Tina was so excited! "Finally someone to love me," she thought. So Tim brought Tina to his home and put her on his shelf. He then went about his life shopping in catalogs looking at other dolls. "Wait!" Tina cried, "What's wrong with me?" But she was too high on the shelf for Tim to hear.

Day after day she sat. Every once in a while Tim would bring her down to play for a minute or so, but he always put her back on her shelf to sit. Tina did everything she could to make herself appealing to Tim, but nothing worked. He still shopped and imagined all the other dolls he could get. Tina cried. She cried for all the lost dreams, all the desires of her heart that were wasting away.

Whenever young men came over to Tim's house they noticed Tina up on the shelf. "You are so lucky," they would say. "Yeah, I know," Tim would say proudly, gazing up at his doll. "Can I play with her?" they would ask. But Tim would stomp his feet and take her off his shelf and say, "No, she is mine!"

"But you don't play with her," they would say.

"I will," Tim would promise. Tina's heart would leap. Instantly she would imagine the fun they were going to have. But then the young men would leave.

"Can we play now?" Tina would beg. Then Tim would smile at Tina—the kind of smile that makes a girl doll's heart flutter. He would say, "Not now," and put her back on the shelf.

Time went by and Tina's hair got dusty, her paint faded and chipped, and still she waited. "No one would want me now," she would cry. But still she was too high for anyone to hear. "Maybe, maybe someday," she would dream.

More time passed and Tim stopped shopping the catalogs

for other dolls he could have. Tina once again became excited, "Maybe now, after all this time, he will want <u>ME</u>." But Tim was tired; he had stopped looking at all.

Tina, the doll up on the shelf, sits and dreams to this day....

Counselor's Corner

It is important that you process your own pain and grief through the questions or statements we provide at the end of each chapter. We encourage you to get a journal to write in as you walk through this book.

❤ *Journal your thoughts concerning the following questions:*

- How can I relate to Tina's Doll Story?

- When have I felt dropped or chipped?

- When have I felt alone in my marriage?

- What dreams have I had dashed by circumstances or unforeseen choices my spouse has made?

Chapter 1
What's Wrong With Me?

There used to be a part of me that wanted to blame all of my hurt, betrayal, and shame on Tim. But through years of counseling and journaling I have come to realize that I came into my marriage already wounded. I have come to realize that my marriage added to the trauma and hurt, but it did not cause it.

I was born the third daughter to a man who only wanted sons. I don't remember him being involved in my life as a child except for little snippets here and there. As I have gotten older and have been seeing some amazing counselors, I am beginning to piece a few of my past memories together—memories of sexual abuse, memories of my father's "porn cabinet," memories of him bringing his many girlfriends home to my mother's house. After he left our family when I was about four years old, I have memories of my mother's drinking, attempted suicides, and abuse. I don't remember my mother hitting me like she did my sisters or my little brother; for some reason, they got the brunt of her anger. I would hear them screaming upstairs and things (and sometimes they) would hit the walls. I would scream from downstairs for it to stop, feeling relieved that I wasn't the one being hit but feeling guilty at the same time. I also remember the names I grew accustomed to: retarded, weak, a liar…I heard a lot of them.

I do have some good memories, like moments when mom's eyes sparkled and we knew she was sober and "in her right mind." But all too soon her eyes would glaze over and we knew to keep our distance. It was a constant game of watching, analyzing, and trying to be perfect. When mom was sober I would try not to leave her side, trying to somehow absorb every bit of love and attention that I could. It was at these times that she would tell me I was perfect and that she never wanted me to grow up.

For the most part, neglect was pretty constant as mom hid in her world of depression, isolation, and alcohol. We all do the best we know how when raising our children; growing up in an alcoholic, abusive family herself coupled with my dad's many affairs and abuse had left my mother terribly wounded. She often told us, "Don't ever trust a man" and "Don't ever need a man." She tried to instill in us that there was nothing we couldn't do as women. She entered us in beauty pageants and modeling school when I was a young teen. I loved the attention and cherished the look of pride on her face when we did well, but I feared the anger she directed at the judges when we did not do well. Desiring to be perfect in order to make my mother proud, I started my battle with anorexia/bulimia.

Mom died from lung cancer during my senior year of high school, leaving me in the care of my stepfather. Around this time I met my first boyfriend. He and I had been dating a few months when my stepfather started asking me intimate questions about my relationship. When he asked if I had had sex yet, I told him that I was waiting until marriage. He laughed at me and asked me the question I had heard so many times before, "What's wrong with you?" Not long after this my stepfather decided I needed to be punished for all the "bad" I did growing up. He called me into his bedroom and made me pull down my pants. He then made me lay across his lap and proceeded to spank me several times. When he was done he told me "all was forgiven."

Weeks followed as I continued to hear the words that would forever haunt me, "What's wrong with you? Why aren't you having sex?" In order to prove there was nothing wrong with me and that I was desirable, I had sex with my virgin boyfriend, both of us breaking the vow that we made to remain pure until marriage. Feeling sick and disgusted with myself as well as manipulated and used, I made myself throw up and vowed never to trust or be vulnerable to any man.

The next few years are a blur of some college, a couple of jobs and a couple of men. I wanted so badly to belong somewhere and to know that I was strong; despite protests from family saying that I was crazy and would never make it, I joined the U.S. Army at the age of 20. After basic training I was sent to my first duty station in Frankfurt, Germany, feeling empowered, strong and free.

It wasn't long after I arrived in Frankfurt that I found myself at local clubs every weekend drinking with fellow service members. Shortly after I started dating a young military man I met at one of these clubs, my unit was sent away on a field exercise. It was here I met a very good-looking officer named Lt. Harris. He was kind and funny and smart. I watched him from a distance, admiring the way he treated others with respect and confidence. We talked a few times, but he was out of my league as both an officer and a gentleman, not to mention the fact that I was already dating someone. After the field exercise I continued to date and sleep with my boyfriend so I decided it might be a good idea to go see a doctor about getting on birth control pills. At this appointment that I found out I was pregnant. In shock and disbelief, I informed my boyfriend of the news. He took it calmly and we started to talk about getting married, but within a couple of weeks, days after my twenty-first birthday, he suggested that perhaps we should consider giving the baby up for adoption. Less than a month later on Christmas Eve, my boyfriend showed up at my barracks with a Christmas present; he told me he was sorry, but he did not love me anymore and did not want to ever see me again. He did, however, offer to pay child support for the baby. I sobbed and he left. I spent Christmas Eve walking the streets of Germany in the rain— cold, wet, alone, and pregnant. The months that followed were filled with rumors and accusations as the offer of child support was withdrawn and replaced with assaults on my character, further strengthening my belief that I should never trust a man.

My labor in the military hospital in Frankfurt, Germany, lasted over eighteen hours; the pain of childbirth didn't hurt near as bad as the pain of being alone. Only a thin curtain separated me from three other women also in labor. I couldn't see any of them, but I could hear their husbands/boyfriends encouraging them and speaking lovingly to them as they cried out in pain. I could hear the men direct the nurses as to what the women needed and the loving anticipation in their voices as they told the women how much they loved them. I craved that kind of love, but I was completely and utterly alone. I was having a baby in a foreign country where I knew almost no one—no one to encourage me, comfort me, or dream about my baby's future with me. No mother, no father, no husband, and no friends; it was just me. And now I was about to have a baby. I was so frightened. I had no idea how to take care of a baby and I had no one to ask.

I brought my beautiful baby girl home to a tiny German apartment where I promised her that I would be the best mom ever. We both spent the first six weeks of her life crying and drinking baby formula given to us by the hospital. After my six-week maternity leave was up, I had to report back to work. After completing paperwork, I took my baby with me to the bowling alley to watch a friend bowl; there was Lt. Harris, bowling with some friends. I sat there watching with my precious baby girl in my lap. Before long he came over and mentioned that he loved to take pictures and had recently purchased a new camera, and could he possibly take pictures of my baby? I gave him my phone number and told him that I would love for him to do that. I didn't expect him to call and was very surprised to hear from him the following morning. A few days later he picked us up in his red Volvo. I did not have a car seat for my baby as I only took public transportation, and to be honest, it didn't really cross my mind that I needed one, until I saw how nervous Tim was driving with me holding my baby in my lap in the back seat. That day Tim took pictures of my baby, made me lunch and talked. He was a wonderful man with such a big heart. Not too long after our first "date" he called and asked me out again. This time when he picked us up he had a beautiful baby car seat securely buckled in the back seat! I was hooked!

After a few more dates, Tim offered to have us stay the night so that he could take me into work the next morning. I agreed so we made a soft pallet on the floor for my baby and I slept in Tim's bed with him. He never even touched me! I was certain that this was the most honorable man I had ever met. This happened several more times; after a bit I began to get a bit concerned. I started again asking myself, *What's wrong with me?* In order to prove that nothing was wrong with me, I eventually came on to Tim. We continued to date for six weeks or so before I got out of the Army on single parent hardship discharge. Tim took us to the airport and cried at our leaving. Inside I was hoping that he would propose to me before we left, but he didn't. So my baby and I headed back home to California. Tim wrote and called often, and his letters were full of feeling and sensuality. I was surprised at how graphic they were, especially since I never felt he was very interested in sex.

Within three months of our leaving, Tim called and asked me to bring my baby back to Germany. He said he missed us too much to live without us. My baby and I flew to Maryland where Tim was visiting with his family; on February 16. 1990, Tim and I got married at a justice of the peace with my baby on my hip. I would love to say that I was in love with Tim and that I dreamed of a "happily-ever-after" but the truth is that I hardly knew Tim at all. I knew he loved my baby and would be a great dad. I knew he would not abuse us and would provide well for us. I didn't know if he really loved me or not, but I figured that if I was always available to him and worked hard at being a good wife, he would grow to love me. Our little family flew back to Germany, and I had no idea what to expect. I didn't know how to be a wife, trust a man, or parent together. All I really knew was that I was supposed to be there for him.

I had heard that men always wanted sex and that most husbands complained that their wives didn't want it enough. I waited, but Tim rarely initiated sex and turned down my attempts quite often. I wondered what happened to the man that I had received all of those sensual letters from. No matter how hard I tried, Tim almost always had an excuse as to why he didn't want sex; he was either too tired or he had a headache. When he did comply, I would feel like he had done me a favor and I would feel cheap and dirty. Most of all, I think I felt defective.

A few months after we were married, Tim accepted an early discharge from the Army with the intention of not having to travel and move as much as he would have in the military. We moved to Pennsylvania, intending to settle down there. I worked as an at-home mom, and within the year was pregnant with our second daughter. Since Tim was offered a job in Texas, a week after our baby was born we moved and bought our first home. Our home life was peaceful, with Tim working hard, traveling continuously, and avoiding me at night. I loved being a mom, but I was so lonely and always wondering what was wrong with me. Was I too fat, too boring, too controlling, too…nothing?

About a year and a half into our marriage, while Tim was on travel with his job, he called to tell me he bought "us" something. When he came home he was pretty excited to show me the "educational" videos he bought. They were called something like "greater sex videos" and they promised better sex and improved intimacy. I agreed to watch them, thinking that I was obviously doing something wrong if my husband didn't want me. I was 23 years old at the time with two small children and I was willing to try anything. The first time we tried to watch one of the videos I became sick to my stomach. I was horrified that people would film this stuff, but I wanted to be wanted, so over time I sat through a couple of them. I hated it and hated Tim for asking me to watch them. Eventually I threw them away, and nothing changed in our marriage.

Thoughts from my journals:

Lord, I am tired of being an afterthought. If only I had a place for the kids and I to go and stay for a while. I know that Tim loves me. I don't think it is a question of love.

After Tim and I had been married for about four years, I badgered him into going to a marriage counselor. Tim didn't have much to say, but after listening to me talk about our sex life the counselor looked at me and asked, "What makes you think that Tim should want sex more than once a month?" My mouth dropped open as I tried to comprehend what this woman was saying to me. Here I had worked up the nerve after four years of not being wanted, convinced Tim that we needed to see someone, and now, with Tim looking on, this woman tells me there isn't a problem, it's just me and my expectations! And there Tim sat, not saying a word, looking completely justified in hearing that it was my problem, just like he had been telling me all these years! I started to cry as our session ended. Tim led me out of the door, trying to comfort me by saying that it was no big deal and we would be fine. I hated him at that moment and felt that I had been completely betrayed.

Tim was a wonderful provider, and made sure that we had everything we needed; the girls have wonderful memories of what a good Dad he was to them when they were younger. But for me looking back at that time, I can't remember Tim ever being there for us, ever really spending time with us. What I remember is the loneliness, the feelings of betrayal, the anger, and the resentment. I remember the way he would yell at the kids and slam his fist on the table or punch at them so close to their little bodies. I remember them saying they love him before they went to bed and him hardly acknowledging them. I remember the kids going up to hug him and him never reaching out to hug them back and him saying things to them like, "What's wrong with you?" I remember him putting stranger's needs far above the needs of our family and him caring more about what others thought about him then whether or not his children knew he loved them. And I remember feeling so guilty for not being happy in my marriage because everyone around me thought that Tim was perfect.

From the very beginning of our marriage Tim was against anything that objectified women. (Or so I thought.) He would not go to strip clubs when his colleagues did, in fact, when a strip club threatened to open up near our home Tim wanted to move. He criticized other men who would look at girly magazines and watch porn videos. He always said how dirty and wrong they were. I began to wonder if he might be gay, which would explain why he hardly ever touched me and why he would rarely look at me when I put on sexy lingerie.

I went from thinking Tim was gay to thinking that he was having an affair. When I was about 6 months pregnant with our third child we were sitting down for lunch at Costco. Tim's eyes became fixated on something as I was talking to him and I could tell he was no longer "with" me. I turned around to see what caught his attention. A woman wearing tight white pants was bending over practicing her golf swing as part of a golfing demonstration. She was obviously enjoying it by the way her hips swayed seductively in front of all the men who were watching; she burst into sexy giggles when she made a mistake.

When I showed him Victoria's Secret catalogues to see if there was anything he thought I should buy, anything he would like to see on me, he would look though the magazine thoughtfully and then say something like, "Honey, I like you in just a t-shirt; these things just make sex cheap." I didn't know at the time that he would later use these images to masturbate.

I worked hard at being a wife and mother, constantly searching books to find out how to be a better wife, anything to tell me how to make my husband desire me. I talked to friends who would complain that their husbands were all over them in bed and that they couldn't even change in front of their husband without him wanting sex. I would go home and look in the mirror to see what was wrong with me. When I changed Tim would look away or leave the room; when I came to bed he would roll over and put his back to me. When I asked for sex, my husband would pull out an excuse from his long list of excuses, and if I touched him in bed he would bristle. I looked for books on the subject, but every one of them was about the wife not wanting sex. All the books I found told the wife that her body was not her own and that she should willingly give it to her husband. Not one book, NOT ONE, addressed the man not wanting sex. I felt completely alone and isolated. What was so wrong with me?

I wish I would have known that there were other women out there like me. I wish I would have known that I was not the only woman whose husband didn't want sex. I wish I would have known that watching a sex video would not help my marriage and that I could/should have said "no." But I believed that maybe I didn't know how to please Tim, and maybe if I learned how to "do it right" he would want me. I believed that my worth as a wife was tied into my desirability as a woman, and that Tim's lack of interest in me sexually proved I was worthless and unlovable and a failure.

I was incredibly lonely. Even when Tim was with me I

usually felt like he was someplace else. If I tried to talk to him about the way I was feeling, he would usually say something that made me feel crazy or stupid and I would walk away wishing that I had never said anything and vowing to keep my feelings to myself. Or he would say that he was too busy, too tired, or any other excuse not to talk with me.

Finally, there came a time when I felt like I had enough. I didn't care if he thought I was crazy; I was tired and lonely and I was done pretending that everything was all right. I decided that instead of talking to him, I would write him a letter shortly before he went on business travel to California. I think that this letter may have had something to do with why he came home so quickly after I told him to stay in California permanently. (You will learn more about that in the next chapter.) I believe he knew that I was serious and that something had to change.

Tim,

Hello. I feel kind of corny writing you a letter, but it seems as though we can't talk lately. I need to share my feelings with you and I need you to pay attention. Please.

First of all... I love my life. I love my home. I love my job and I love my family. I am at the point in my life where I see how fast time flies and how little time we really have with our children. I am starting to see how little time we have with our health, our bodies, and our sexiness.

I feel like I am a relatively good mom, but as a wife I feel like a failure. I know that you love me, but I don't think you like me very much and, truthfully, it wouldn't surprise me to find out that you had a girlfriend somewhere. Make fun of me if you want—or feel convicted—that is the way I feel.

It's not the travel. You say that that is necessary, and I believe you. You work hard because it is rewarding and necessary and it is your job. BUT you show us in no uncertain terms that you don't like being with us. When the girls try to hug you, you usually push them away or pretend to get hurt. I can't tell you how many times I've been asked by one or more of the girls why daddy had so many kids if he doesn't like to be around them. The older ones KNOW that you can't wait until they are old enough to move out. You make it very clear in your jokes and comments to them and to other people.

You provide wonderfully. We HAVE everything that we could ever need. You are not abusive and I know that you love us in your own way. But I feel as though you keep us all at arms reach. And you make me feel like a burden.

Tim, I want so badly to feel wanted. I am still young and I try to always be attractive to you. But you are so tired that as soon as I go to put the girls to bed at night, you are gone into your world of computer or TV. When exactly do you expect to build a relationship with the older girls? You are never available to them and when you are around you complain that you are tired and go spend hours on the computer. And they are left wondering what is wrong with them.

I want to be kissed again. I want to be desired. Blame our lack of sex on anything you want. No time alone? If you go to bed at nine and fall asleep to the TV, what do you expect? I tried to make time alone last year. We went away without the kids. Remember? And out of the two days that we were gone you spent one day with me and went fishing the other with your brother all day, leaving me alone to follow your sister around. Do you know how hard it was to leave the kids for two days? And I did it because you said that our lack of sex and intimacy was because we never spent time together. But it is not me that you want to be alone with. You also say it because I am still nursing the baby. I could wean her for you so that we could be together more, but I know that nothing would change. And then I would resent you. I know that these are just excuses; they are not the truth.

So I am left not knowing what to do. What do you want? I

get the feeling that you would be so much happier alone. And that is a terrible feeling.

I love you more today than when we were first married. But I do not like the feeling of being where I am not wanted. And I don't want the girls to feel pushed away anymore either.

I don't know where I'd go or what I would do, but if you need space, then I will go. I will take the girls and go. Or...are you planning on going away again on travel? Why don't you just go now? Decide what you want. I would rather be alone and lonely with you gone than alone and lonely with you here. The latter is getting too hard on me.

When we saw that counselor in Texas many years ago, (the one who asked me why I thought that we should be having sex more than once a month and that it was my problem wanting it more and I just needed to get over it) remember how we stood outside on her balcony afterwards and I was crying? You said we just needed to talk more. But now when I try to talk to you, you say, It's too early, I haven't fully woken up yet," or "It's too late, I want to go to bed now," or "We can't talk when the kids are around."

Like I said earlier, I've realized how short life is and how quick youth passes you by. I am still young and I need to feel young, loved, and desired. You may hate to kiss me and you may cringe at the idea of being intimate with me, but I am tired of feeling like just a mother and a housekeeper. I need to be somebody's' wife. I need to feel like you want me around not just to take care of you and our children, but because you enjoy me and love me.

If you can't, or don't want to, then let me know and I will leave. The kids and I will find somewhere else to live and leave you exactly where you want to be. Alone.

Tina

As difficult as this letter was to write, this was the turning point for me. I realized I had a voice and, regardless of the outcome, I had to speak the truth. Looking back, I wish I had had a group of women who could have validated my feelings and supported me in this decision.

Counselor's Corner

You may be in Tina's situation where you feel all alone. Sadly, Tina had to navigate through her journey without the help of others. Finding her voice was a huge step towards healing for her. If you feel alone in your journey, I encourage you to seek some sort of support with women who understand your pain. Betrayal & Beyond groups, found in many locations across the United States, have tools to help you on this difficult journey. (Go to puredesire.org, click on "get help," and enter your zip code to see if there is a group near you.) Also, I encourage you, like Tina, to *journal your trauma history.*

Dr. Patrick Carnes surveyed over a thousand sex addicts and their partners and discovered that high percentages of both experienced abuse prior to marriage.[1]

Abuse	Addicts	Partners of Sex Addicts
Emotional Abuse	97%	91%
Physical Abuse	72%	71%
Sexual Abuse	81%	81%

As we will see in later chapters, this is not an excuse for the addict's behaviors and choices, but it will help us to see how early trauma and coping mechanisms developed at an early age affect our choices as adults. This is not only true for your spouse, but also for you. In order to survive Tina's growing up years, she created some vows: "I have to be perfect in order to be accepted." Also notice the haunting vows that her mom projected to her: "Don't ever trust a man," "Don't ever need a man." From Tina's husband's avoidance of sexual behavior, she began to believe, *There must be something wrong with me.* These are lies the enemy wants us to believe. We can't change our trauma history but we can change the lies and vows we have made as a result of it.

Journal some lies you might have believed from your trauma history.

The *Betrayal & Beyond* workbooks (published by Pure Desire) help you discover the lies you have believed. When Tina began her healing journey she didn't realize Tim had an addiction and she also didn't understand that sexual addiction can cause the addict to be sexual with himself and sexually anorexic with his spouse. He has trained his brain to isolate and connect sexually with images rather than a real person. Because this usually starts in his early teens, true intimacy is scary for him. He has usually believed the lie that in some way he is "worthless" or "less than" because of being rejected or abandoned in his past. Therefore, to be sexual with himself or even have anonymous sex is less intimidating than risking rejection from the closest person to him, his wife. The *Seven Pillars of Freedom for Men* by Ted Roberts helps the addict to discover the source of his woundedness that is driving the sexual addiction.

❤ ***Journal some of the lies your husband may believe because of his own trauma history.***

Seven Pillars of Freedom for Men helps men get in touch with those lies by asking them to list their ten most hurtful memories and what they believe about themself in light of those memories.

Chapter 2

Surviving the First Stages of Discovery

The only thing that would ever cause me to leave my husband is if he had an affair! Famous last words! Clarify an affair for me. Is it an affair if your husband looks at other women and later masturbates to the photos he takes in his mind? Is it an affair when he avoids sex with you because he already "took care of himself" while looking at images of other women on the computer? Or is it just an affair when there is an actual woman involved? Jesus said, "But I tell you that anyone who looks at a woman lustfully has already committed adultery with her in his heart" (Matthew 5:28 NIV). According to God, it is ALL adultery. And it all hurts. Bad.

Through the years Tim and I had been to a few counselors. One said I was too controlling; another one said I was too mothering, and added, "Who would want to sleep with their mother?" It seemed that it was always me, and he would just silently sit there listening to the counselor as if he had no idea that there was a problem. Did he not know that inside I wanted to die? Did he not know they were tearing me down to my very core? Couldn't he say something, anything, to defend me? But he just sat there while I shriveled up inside. Then we would go home and pretend like nothing happened. I was so confused, and jealous of all my friends who couldn't keep their husbands off of them. What was so wrong with me?

For 18 years this went on. I played games with myself, such as deciding that not only would I not initiate sex anymore, but also if he tried to come on to me, I would say no! Maybe if he thought he couldn't have me he would want me more. Brilliant plan! But it didn't work. And I would feel even worse. I tried sexy lingerie and talking dirty; I even tried dancing on the bed one Christmas in a sexy Santa suit. I put on the song *Santa Baby* and danced on the bed as sexy as I could. I felt so vulnerable and stupid up on that bed! Tim came in, watched for a second or two, laughed at me, and then turned and left the room. I could hear him out in the living room with the girls laughing and talking about Christmas. I was heartbroken.

I told myself I just had to get closer to God and then I wouldn't need sex. I could care less about the sex! I just so badly wanted Tim to want me. Sex was the only thing that I felt "just I" could give him. The girls loved him; he had friends that he joked around with. Sex was the only thing that I didn't have to share with anyone else. It was "just ours." WHAT WAS WRONG WITH ME????

Then one day a friend confided in me that her husband was addicted to pornography. I was appalled! *What a dirty man!* I thought. I told her that she should leave him. I told her he had committed adultery and that she had every right to leave him. I told her that if my husband ever did that I would be out of there. She cried and told me I was right, she knew I was right; she just loved him so much. I told her I would pray for her. When I got off the phone, I thanked my husband for being so opposed to that "stuff," feeling very lucky that my only problem was that my husband didn't want sex. Little did I know that within the next year I would find myself in the same situation. My advice here: *Be careful what measure you use to judge. You WILL be measured by it!* (Matthew 7:2-my paraphrase)

God has a way of bringing our sin into the light. Tim had taken a job in California for six months while the girls and I remained at our house in Pennsylvania, with the plan that we would join him in California in a few months for the summer break. But after he left I noticed I felt more peaceful and I liked myself so much more. I didn't have to hush the kids all of the time; I didn't have to wonder when he was coming to bed or if we might have sex that night. Nobody questioned my parenting and I didn't have to constantly make excuses to the kids about why daddy was so tired and grumpy. It was then that I realized that I didn't want to live like that anymore. I knew that I could not afford to live alone with six children but if Tim was willing to stay in California and live there permanently as though he were single (which is what I thought he wanted all along), then the kids and I could just stay in Pennsylvania. We wouldn't get a divorce; Tim could just live however he wanted and not have to answer to me. He would never have to sleep with me again and I would be free from always feeling like I was doing something wrong!

The next time Tim and I talked I told him I was done. I was done being in a loveless, sexless, lonely marriage. I was done with his constant travel; I was just DONE. I told him I wanted him to stay in California alone and that the girls and I would stay in our home. I assured him that I did not want a divorce, I was just tired of trying so hard. Tim's response? He told me I was stupid and crazy and he hung up the phone.

The next morning Tim showed up at the bottom of the stairs; he had taken the red-eye flight home. On one hand I was pleased that he had come home, but on the other hand I felt angry and betrayed, that my feelings and desires had no value. After talking things through, Tim and I tried to have sex. It felt like he was forcing himself to engage in sex, very robotic and cold. I felt like running away, almost panicky as though I was being held down. My mind was racing; I was certain that Tim was having an affair and that he had just left his lover. I was completely disgusted at the idea that he had probably just left another woman and now was trying to have sex with me. I felt dirty, cheap, and thrown away. When it was obvious that Tim was not going to be able to continue, I assured him that it was fine and excused myself to go and get ready for the day. Tim went into the bathroom to take a bath so I followed him and questioned him about his activities at the hotel. When I asked if he was having an affair, he laughed and accused me of being "nuts" Since he was now in the bathtub and was a captive audience I decided to question him further. When I asked him about pornography, he indignantly told me to "stop making things up to be mad about." (Over the years I had learned I had to ask a question in just the right way in order to get the answer I was looking for. The question had to be very specific with no wiggle room or he would manipulate his way out of answering honestly without actually lying.)

I continued to think of ways to ask that would prompt him to tell me what was going on. But finally, I just got tired of trying. I told him I knew that there was something going on and unless he told me what it was, I would just have to assume that he was having an affair and I would leave and take the kids with me. I told him that I didn't think that there was anything wrong with masturbating and that everyone did it once in a while. He then told me that he used to every once in a while when he was a kid and that he sometimes did it when he was on business travel. I thanked him for being honest, left the bathroom, then I sat on the bed and thought about what he just told me. *Sometimes while on travel.* Then I started to remember…I remembered the stuff I would sometimes find around the toilet when I cleaned the bathroom, the stuff in the shower that I always wondered about. (Did he blow his nose in the shower?) I thought about how many times he would take showers before bed and how long they were, all the while I would be lying in bed waiting for him. And then how he would come to bed and turn his back to me and fall asleep. All of sudden it hit me: Tim masturbated instead of having sex with me! I was so angry I started to pace. I didn't know what to do with my anger and years of pent up frustration. On the other hand, I wasn't sure if I had a right to be angry at all. Was this just what men did? Was it normal? Was it acceptable? I didn't know and I needed to think.

I packed an overnight bag got into the car and drove away. I called Tim to tell him that I had left and I needed time and space to think. He insisted that I stop somewhere and talk to him, so I met him in a nearby parking lot. As he pulled his car alongside of mine I hopped out of the car and spoke to him through his passenger window. I told him I knew that he was masturbating instead of sleeping with me. He denied it, but the look on his face told me otherwise. He reminded me of a caged animal looking for a way out, but knows he is caught. I told him that I did not believe him and I couldn't live with him lying to me. He got very angry and told me that yes, he did masturbate, but just once in a while, and it wasn't that big of a deal. I sensed there was way more to it, but he refused to discuss it any further; I responded that I needed time to think, got back into my car, and drove away.

All day I just drove, cried, and prayed. I stopped at churches to cry in their parking lots and gas stations to use their bathrooms. I wrote in my journal and I cried some more. Tim called several times while I was out, but I just could not bring myself to answer the phone. What would I say? How could I tell him how hurt and scared I was? I ended up at a park and I prayed. Thoughts flooded my mind, the biggest of which was, *What else don't I know?*

I was worn out, confused, and scared. Now evening, I just wanted to go home and be with my babies; I wanted all of this "mess" to go away. The next time Tim called I picked up the phone. He was kind and gentle and loving and I wanted him to come hold me and make it all go away so badly, so I told him where I was and he drove over to meet me. When he got to the park he seemed so afraid and vulnerable. He said he was sorry with such sincerity; I couldn't help but believe him. He said he never dreamed it would bother me so much, and it would never happen again because he knows that it hurt me so badly. After he said he would rather die than live without me, he cried like I have never heard him cry before, begged me to forgive him, and said we could work through this together. I was overwhelmed by his remorse and vulnerability. I started to feel guilty for putting him through this and I wondered if I was just making a big deal out of something that was insignificant. Before we left the park that night Tim prayed with me. I think this was the first time he had ever prayed anything but a food blessing with me. He prayed and asked God to help him to stop "like I've asked You so many times before." He has been talking to God about this all this time? He has felt guilty enough to talk to God about it and I never knew? I cried for his pain. I cried for the guilt he had lived with all this time and I never even knew. How can you live with someone for 18 years and not know? "Lord help us through this," I prayed.

The next day when we met with a counselor I was afraid that he, like all the others, would say it was my fault. And then Tim would be off the hook once again and nothing would change. But I was also excited. I was excited because we had a place to start. And maybe this time we could fix it.

The counselor told us that Tim had a sexual addiction that probably went back to his childhood. He said he probably started masturbating as a way to comfort himself when he was feeling alone or rejected, and that when those same feelings came up now Tim would go to the thing he knew would comfort him. He recommended Tim read a book titled *Every Man's Battle.*[2] In the back of the book was a phone number to New Life. This phone number was the beginning of our healing and it soon became my link to reality.

Some books that I read during this time made me feel that God had put me in this marriage as a way to punish me, that my purpose in life was to be there to support Tim and allow him to live however he wanted and I was just supposed to stand beside him, forgive him, and pray for him. I felt completely trapped. If I decided to stay with Tim and help him through this, I was risking being walked on; if I decided to leave him I was being a very unforgiving Christian. I was haunted by the many times I had heard that Christians were called to "forgive and forget," and I wondered why God hated me so much as to allow me to continue to feel unloved and rejected my entire life. I felt like a horrible Christian, an unloving wife, and a horrible lover. I couldn't stop crying and thought I was going crazy. I was afraid I would say the wrong thing and make things worse. I didn't know what to do or say. All I wanted to do was to hold Tim and tell him I loved him. I wanted so badly to step back in time and hold the little boy in him that felt so lonely and rejected that he had to go "there." I wanted to tell that little boy in him that I would always love him and be there for him. I ached inside for Tim. But I also hated him. I hated him with a passion that I never thought possible. I wanted him out of my life and I wanted to make him hurt as much as I did. I was so confused and crazy-feeling. And what if the counselor was wrong about Tim having an addiction? What if this was just another lie to throw me off track and was just another excuse? I was so confused!

Thoughts from my journals:

Doesn't Tim know how much I love him? How much I value him? How smart I think he is, and how handsome? How can you truly have a relationship with someone when you have such a secret? It affects everything. When you feel guilty about something you act guilty. And then you cover it up with more lies. How many lies has he told? He says he doesn't see how it could affect our relationship. How can he not see it? If he masturbates, he doesn't want sex with me. All these years of wondering why he didn't want me! How could he let me cry myself to sleep so many nights?

I cried a lot over the next few days. Tim was getting impatient with my tears. He got angry and told me that this was exactly why he never told me in the first place. Now I felt guilty, I did something wrong again! I was so afraid to do anything, I just wanted to die, to end this pain and make it all go away. I went for a walk to think. *How easy it would be to trip in front of one of these trucks, then the pain would go away. If I got real hurt, Tim would see my pain; if I died, Tim would be able to move on. He could remarry and start all over again, fresh. And my kids would be better off with someone who could handle things better.* By the grace of God, I made it home safe. When I got home, Tim was in the living room watching a movie with our girls. They were all laughing at the movie and I was hurt that they didn't seem to even notice that I was gone. I hated Tim all the more that he could just sit there and watch a movie while I was hurting so bad—while I was wishing that I were dead. How can life just continue to go on as though nothing happened? With no one to talk to and no desire to pretend that nothing was going on, I went back to reading my book on healing. One of the stories told of a woman, who, upon hearing of her husband's addiction, said, "At least you were thinking about me when you did it." Then she found out he wasn't thinking about her at all! Right then it hit me! It's not me! He had been thinking about other women all this time! *Who? Did I know them? Was he thinking about them when he was with me?* I was so angry! I couldn't eat much, and what I did eat wouldn't stay in. How was I ever going to survive this?

Some thoughts from my journals:

I feel so overwhelmed with junk right now! How do these women just not die!

The books can say all they want about the husband's pain! It's sick, it's horrible, it's perverted!

If it wasn't for my children I would just want to die!

If you can identify with what I have shared so far, the only thing that I can recommend is to get help—for you and for your husband. He needs Every Man's Battle, a Pure Desire Group, or a treatment facility as soon as possible. Every Man's Battle is a biblically based three-day workshop offered by New Life Ministries for men who are looking for God's wisdom in keeping themselves sexually pure. This wonderful resource can help your husband realize that he has an addiction and equip him with the necessary tools to begin to overcome his addiction. As Stephen Arterburn points out in the introduction to *Pure Desire* by Dr. Ted Roberts, Pure Desire Ministry picks up where New Life leaves off. A Pure Desire group will give him true accountability using biblical and clinical tools; these groups are also designed to help him discover the reason he is medicating his pain with sexual activity. The Pure Desire website also recommends Christian counselors who are trained in trauma and sexual addiction (IITAP Counselors).

Right now he is probably vulnerable and afraid, so now is the time he will most likely do anything for you. Find yourself someone to talk to, not just anyone, but someone that you can trust. Please try not to be surprised if they are shocked and respond in disgust like I did when my dear, hurting friend called me. Just know that it is called *EVERY Man's Battle* for a reason. In the next chapter you will see that 68-70% of men sitting in the church this weekend are in sexual bondage. Many wives would be surprised to find out that their husband may be one of them. You are not alone. I remember being worried about what other women would think if I told them about Tim. Looking back, I can see patterns in their husbands that were quite similar to Tim's. You do not have to walk this alone. Find a Betrayal & Beyond group through Pure Desire Ministries or some other woman's support group so that you have the support of other women who understand sexual addiction.

Pray a lot. Yell and scream at God if you must. Jesus questioned God while he hung on the cross. He asked, "Why?" You CAN ask why. God knows your pain. Isaiah 53:3 states that Jesus would be "a man of sorrows, and familiar with suffering."

Journaling was very helpful to me at this time as well. I could tell my journal anything: how mad I was, how much I hated my husband, how afraid I was that the pain would never go away. Recently I have reread all my journal entries from this time period. I cried many tears over the overwhelming incredible pain and over my loneliness when I didn't know what to do or where to turn. But I have also been able to see the path toward healing that God brought me through, the long and windy path that you are now on. And I have rejoiced at the victory and healing that I have found on this path, the same victory and healing that I wish for you. It is possible. You will be able to breathe again; you will be able to love again. With God's help, you will make it to the other side of this. I know it hurts worse than anything you ever thought you would go through, and no, it isn't fair. God does want better for you. He wants you to feel the love that he created marriage to give you. Please know that there are so many women right where you are and there is nothing any of them could have done to prevent their husband's sin. IT IS NOT YOUR FAULT. IT IS NOT ABOUT YOU. I know that it probably feels like it is, but it's not. And that is a very hard concept to grasp. It was for me as well. It is for every woman. Just trust me here; IT IS NOT ABOUT YOU.

Counselor's Corner

Tina brings up an important truth in this chapter. Your spouse's addiction is not your fault. He brought his pain and how he medicates that pain into the marriage. In our counseling offices, we have found that more than 80% of men struggling with sexual addiction carry a deep father wound and all of them have some sense of feeling worthless. This began in their family of origin; as a young person or teen they learned to medicate their pain with porn and masturbation. This addiction helps them to temporarily push their pain away or compartmentalize the pain. Because it has been less threatening to bond to an image rather than a real woman who can reject or wound them further, their behavior often escalates in marriage because they fear intimacy. So many men think marriage will solve their masturbation problem. But as we say in our *Sexy Christians* book and seminars:

> We must understand that our struggles don't all disappear when we come to Christ. They don't all end on our wedding day either. In fact, it seems as though the struggles increase because we're suddenly confronted at close range by issues we never knew existed....we marry our patient and our healer.[3]

Because of the fall of Adam and Eve, men and women have issues. If these issues aren't dealt with we end up doing the tango from hell rather than the waltz from heaven that God intended.

True intimacy requires we become close and uncomfortable. Allowing someone else to "see into me" is not always comfortable. The addict has learned to avoid that at all cost because he feels flawed (worthless) and intimacy poses a huge threat to the double life he has created and has brought into the marriage. We will look further at the double life in later chapters and discover how addiction affects the addict's thinking at an early age.

- ❤ *Journal how you relate to Tina's emotional ups and downs.*

- ❤ *Journal how you might be able to relate to dancing the tango from hell you have been doing with your spouse. Include how you have experienced a lack of intimacy.*

- ❤ *Write a prayer that cries out to God for what you would like your marriage to become. What would the waltz from heaven look like to you?*

Chapter 3
What Is Porn Addiction?

When I found out about Tim's sexual addiction I wanted to know the facts about sex addiction. Somehow knowing more about it all made it easier to deal with. Looking at it from a clinical perspective seemed to help me, so I have decided to give you some facts about sexual addiction and porn.

According to Stephen Arterburn in his book *When You Love Too Much,*

> Sex for the sex addict becomes like a drug, and like any drug, it is used to deaden pain: the pain of rejection, loneliness, fear, anxiety, childhood abuse or any of a dozen other hurts. But it doesn't work. Sex masks the pain for a moment, providing a brief mood change. The short-lived relief comes not just from the orgasm, but also the ritual leading up to it—the seeking, which becomes the central organizing factor of daily life. But in the long run, instead of making the pain better, it ends up making it worse as the person experiences deepening humiliation and loss of control over his or her life.[4]

He goes onto say,

> Recovering sex addicts invariably look back in disbelief that they were capable of the behaviors that characterized them at the height of their addiction. They can see clearly in retrospect how much they

wanted to be loved and accepted. Seeking relief from the pain of rejection, they betrayed their values, their morals and their very selves. Having been rejected by others, they came to reject themselves over the very behaviors they could not stop. Seeking acceptance, they ended up isolated from everyone.[5]

Next I would like to tell you about the cycle of addiction. Stephen Arterburn points out in *When You Love Too Much* that the phases of the addictive cycle are easy to see from the outside, but almost impossible to discern from the inside. He states, "Sex addicts are usually laboring under their own denial, so deeply trapped in the addictive cycle that they cannot see any way of escape."[6]

Let's look at Stephen Arterburn's description of the addictive cycle[7], with my comments following his explanation of each phase in the cycle.

Obsession: Sex addiction begins with a severe focus on self. Unable to concentrate on daily life the addict feels compelled to find relief as soon as possible.

If the girls would start to giggle or play too loudly, Tim would always yell at them to "shut-up." He was intolerant of tears and extremely sensitive to the sound of children. I remember one of my daughters asking me one day why daddy had so many children if he didn't want them. In a video I recorded when my children were younger, they are dancing, spinning, and laughing to Christmas music in the living room. From somewhere behind me you can hear Tim yell at them that they are making too much noise. The camera pans to where the voice is coming from and there is Tim playing a war game on his computer, completely removed and seemingly unaware of the joy he just sabotaged in the other room. I realize now he couldn't be present in the moment. He had trained his brain to find comfort in obsessing with things that would remove him from living in the here and now.

The Hunt: The sex addict looks for something or someone with which to express his or her sexual desires. This hunt is often highly ritualized.

Most nights I went to bed alone and waited for Tim to join me. I would try to make myself smell nice "just in case." Some time later he would come upstairs and either take a shower or climb into bed and put his back to me. If I indicated in any way that I wanted to be intimate he would make some excuse, get irritated, or pretend to be asleep. Days before Tim would go on business trips, we would almost always get into a fight. I used to think that it was my fault because I was insecure about him leaving and me being alone. I have come to realize that this was one way that Tim could justify his use of pornography while away. In his subconscious mind, the excuse for the hunt had already begun before he even left the house.

Recruitment: The addict identifies and obtains a victim. If he is acting out with porn, he will usually seek out a particular type of porn. Often, the type will change and escalate so he can get a bigger high.

Gratification: Orgasm, either by masturbation or intercourse.

Return to Normal: "After the fantasy is fulfilled and orgasm achieved, the obsession lifts and the addict once again feels 'normal.'"[8]

I realize now that Tim went through predictable cycles; everything seemed fine for awhile and I would think things were good. Then some stress would happen and Tim would change. I always assumed that I was just handling things wrong and if I would just be more understanding things would be fine. Tim would start talking about moving (which we did about every three years) and then he would become increasingly irritable. He would spend more and more time on the computer and within a few weeks things would return to normal.

Justification: Once the addict becomes aware of what he or she has done, they try to justify it.

A few days before Tim would go away on his business trips he would be incredibly irritable and inevitably we would fight. I always thought that he was trying not to miss us or that I was doing something to irritate him. I would want to have sex before he left (sort of an "insurance policy") but he would be "too angry." Now I know that it was all a part of his addiction. He could go away on his trip and feel fully justified watching and masturbating to porn because I was not meeting his needs. All of this behavior is self-focused with no thought of a real and intimate relationship.

Blame: The addict will look for someone to blame rather than take responsibility for what he or she has done.

I have shared how when we went to counseling he made it sound like I was the problem rather than revealing what was really going on. I felt he and the counselor were blaming me for the problem. If I confronted Tim on his irritability or his anger, he would quite often tell me that I was making things up. He would say things that made me feel like I was going crazy, even to the point of calling me crazy.

Shame: "As the addict finds it increasingly difficult to project onto others what he or she has done, guilt and shame set in and eat away at the addict's soul. The individual feels bad, less for what he or she has *done* than for what he or she has *become*."

Especially as I think about at Tim's growing up years, I know he felt worthless. Not being able to stop his sexual behavior was in direct conflict with his Christian values, and I can see now that he felt more shame and more like a failure.

Despair: The addict feels hopeless to change.

Tim finally mentioned he had tried many times to stop the cycle but was unsuccessful; he was feeling hopeless and would quickly move to the next stage and decide to try harder.

Promises: The addict promises that he will never go to "that place" again. "The addict's promises serve only to refocus his or her obsessive thinking and trigger the addictive process yet again."[9]

And so the cycle continues because he has not been given tools to deal with changing the cycle. The main reason this cycle isn't broken is the isolation of most addicts, including Tim. The enemy has tricked them into thinking they are the only Christians struggling with this issue, and they must be worthless because their faith doesn't work for them. This adds to the shame and keeps the cycle going.

Over 3,000 data points from Evangelical Churches across the USA compiled by Pure Desire Ministries show:[10]

- 68-70% of men sitting in church this weekend are in sexual bondage. They are not just struggling; they are addicted.

- 40% of women who are on the internet are involved with cyber-sex.

- 24-30 % of women attending church are in sexual bondage.

- The fastest growing population using porn on the internet are 12-17 year olds.

Other statistics show what is happening in the general population. These help us to understand the difficulty of the battle for sexual purity. In his article, *Porn Stats*, Craig Gross compiled the following statistics:[11]

- 12% of the websites on the Internet are pornographic. That's at least 24,644,172 sites.

- Every second, $3,075.64 is being spent on pornography and 28,258 Internet users are viewing porn.

- 40 million Americans are regular visitors to porn sites.

- 70% of men aged 18-24 visit porn sites in a typical month.

- In the US, Internet porn pulls in $2.84 billion per year. The entire worldwide porn industry is worth $4.9 billion.

- 25% of all search engine requests are pornography related. That's about 68 million a day.

- 35% of all internet downloads are pornographic.

- 34% of internet users have experienced unwanted exposure to porn either through pop up ads, misdirected links, or emails.

- There are 116,000 searches for "child pornography" every day.

- The average age at which a child first sees porn online is 11.

- 20% of men admit to watching porn online at work. The average porn site visit lasts 6 minutes and 29 seconds.

- The most popular day of the week for viewing porn is Sunday.

I realize that these statistics are overwhelming, but I wanted you to see just how big the problem is and how Christians are being influenced by the world. Realize, it is not just your husband; it truly is every man's battle.

I remember feeling like my entire world was a lie. I didn't know what to believe or where to turn. I believed my marriage was a complete sham, my husband was a pervert and a fraud, and I was a fool. I hated my husband with a hate I never thought possible, yet I loved him more than I could explain or understand. I was confused, scared, hurt, and shocked. I wanted him to hurt as bad as I did, and yet the Christian in me said that I should forgive him. The Scripture about looking at the speck in your brother's eye when you have a plank in your own (Matthew 7:5) was making me feel guilty for all of the negative emotions I was experiencing. Trust me, if you are feeling like I was—you are not alone. I have read countless blogs and websites where women have written about their husband's addiction and they all say the same thing, they all seem to feel the same way. Every woman is hurt and afraid, and almost every woman is angry. There are a few who say they are not angry and that we need to "get over it" and forgive. Yes, we are to forgive, but quick forgiveness is sometimes excusing a behavior; if we excuse a behavior we are then set up to have it happen again. Give yourself permission to take it slowly and allow yourself time to process the damage.

Forgiving too quickly may also be an attempt to make it go away, but it doesn't just go away. It gets stored as a feeling that will come up again and again until we deal with it. Look at the Old Testament, especially the book of Hosea. God was hurt and He was angry. His people had betrayed Him and He likened them to a harlot. Later He offers forgiveness, but first he felt the pain of betrayal. We are the same way.

Please know that your marriage probably is not a lie. The problem is part of your marriage, not all of it. He didn't maliciously set out to hurt you. In fact, he may not have even been consciously aware that it would hurt you at all. Your spouse may deny he has a problem; ask him to go to the Pure Desire website and take the SAST (Sexual Addiction Screening Test). Have him answer yes to any questions if they have ever been true in his life. If he answers yes to six of the first twenty questions he is an addict. He may not be acting out now (he may be like a dry drunk) but his brain has been changed. This evaluation helps break his denial.

In his book *When You Love Too Much,* Steven Arterburn points out the brain problem by sharing some of the ingrained thinking addicts have: "Love holds the possibility of rejection or disappointment. The masturbator finds it easier to fall back on self-gratification. What seems like a harmless habit becomes a trap that blocks out others and forces the addict to suffer alone."[12] Thus, in his mind intimacy with a real woman is too risky; he might be rejected. As a Christian he has probably tried to stop but hasn't been able to do so, despite destructive results and deep feelings of shame.

Dr. Ted Roberts, pastor and sexual addiction therapist, says that it is easier for a cocaine addict to overcome a cocaine addiction than it is for a porn addict to overcome his addiction because porn is always accessible and the images stay in their mind. Unlike the cocaine or alcohol addicts, porn addicts do not have needle tracks or leave bottles lying around. The denial structure is huge, but it is possible for them to overcome it. Through becoming part of a group and breaking isolation, and possibly counseling with someone who understands sexual addiction, your husband CAN overcome this. Dr. Roberts further points out every piece of armor shared in Ephesians 6 refers to the brain; the battle is in the mind. As men join groups and go through the Pure Desire material, they acquire tools to begin to renew their minds as Romans 12:2 challenges us to do: *Don't be conformed to this world but be transformed by the renewing of your mind.*

I had such a difficult time understanding how Tim could love me and masturbate to porn at the same time. I wondered what could cause him to go to porn in the first place. I will attempt to offer answers to both questions. The first question being how he could view porn knowing that I was in bed waiting for him. To a man who views pornography frequently, the women he views aren't women in the way that wives are. They are air brushed images. The women in *Playboy* are called "bunnies" making them toys to be played with. Women in car and motorcycle magazines who are draped over a car are "property" to be bought and sold like the vehicles they are sprawled over. Sports magazines will have a swimsuit edition, which makes women a sport to be played, scored, and conquered. These images are designed to feed your husband's fantasy life. Addicts live in fantasy because they have trained their brain to escape real life and the real world. At an early age, the enemy uses porn to capture the addict's imagination and make him believe that life is too hard and this little bit of pleasure will help him deal with stress, disappointment, and the fears he faces. It soon becomes a habit; now when stressors come he has trained his brain to crave porn.

You, on the other hand, are his wife. You have value and worth. He loves you and would never think of you in that way. Even when a man takes a "visual snapshot" of a woman and then masturbates to the image, even then he puts her in one of the situations in his mind that makes her an object to be played. Those images help him to avoid real intimacy. Usually in his past he has learned that if you get too close to someone they will hurt you. Porn soothes whatever problem he is medicating and helps him avoid risking real intimacy.

Tim lived in a fantasy world that did not include me. The thought of me wearing lingerie was a threat to him and would force him to deal with his fantasy life. If he could keep the two different worlds going at the same time—where neither one ever met the other—that would keep him safe.

Now for the second question about why men go to porn in the first place. It used to be thought that in order for a man to become addicted to porn he had to have been molested or rejected as a child. This is definitely one of the reasons that some men turn to porn, but not the only reason. Some men go there when they are young because they are lonely or because they long for love, closeness, and unconditional acceptance that they might not otherwise be getting at home. It is also a way for a man to find validation, for in the fantasy of pornography, unlike in real life, there is no criticism, real or imagined, of male performance. Unlike real life, the pornographic world is a place where men find their authority unchallenged and in which women are their willing and even grateful servants. And then, some men, unaware of the addictive power of pornography, fall prey to its enslavement later in life. That is one reason why Scripture so clearly states in Proverbs 4:28, "Above all else, guard your heart, for it is the wellspring of life."

Some men turn to porn as a means to control. When they are young, some men may feel very out of control in the world in which they are growing up. If dad is never home or available and mom is controlling or absent, a young boy may turn to porn because it is something that he *can* control. He can control the women and he can control his body, but eventually pornography, instead of being something that men control, becomes a source of bondage. Men masturbate to pornography and eventually become addicted to the fantasy life that it provides.

When Tim met me in the park that day he prayed and asked God to help him not to "act out" anymore. He then added, "like I've asked so many times before." This touched my heart so deeply to know that not only did he agree that it was very wrong, but he also was willing to go to God about it. I also knew by his prayer that he really did want to stop. At first I wasn't sure if I believed him or not. But if his prayer was truly heartfelt, then I was deeply moved. I now know, years later, that his prayer did come from his heart. I wish I would have known this back then. It would have given me a foundation on which to start rebuilding our marriage, but because I wasn't sure what truth was anymore, I chose to distrust everything that he said until it was proven to be true. This is perfectly normal, so don't beat yourself up if you don't trust anything that he says for a while.

But back to what I was saying about his prayer. In the research that I have done these past few years I have found a common thread among the men who are struggling with sexual addiction: most of them hate their addiction and most of them say that after they have "acted out" they are left feeling more lonely and isolated. They are disgusted with themselves, they vow never ever to do it again, then they go back into their everyday lives with new resolve. Before long the cycle of addiction starts all over again. When an addict starts down the path towards acting on his addiction, his brain doesn't think about the consequences of the sin; all the addict knows is that this is a place to feel loved and accepted and significant, even if it is just for a moment. The truth is, however, most men loathe the person in them who goes there. They are just not properly equipped or trained as to how to break free from their addiction.

I wish I would have known what was true and what was not. I wish someone could have told me how long it would take for Tim to get better. I wish someone could have told me how to tell if he was acting out or not. I wish I believed that he loved me back then and that he was just as scared and as confused as I was.

Your husband *can* find healing. Jesus lived out the prediction of Isaiah 53:4: "He took our infirmities and bore our diseases."

The truth about your man's addiction WILL be revealed. Jesus said, "There is nothing concealed that will not be disclosed, nothing hidden that will not be made known" (Matthew 10:26).

Your husband probably hates his sin as much as Paul hated his sin:

> [15] *I do not understand what I do. For what I want to do I do not do, but what I hate I do.* [16] *And if I do what I do not want to do, I agree that the law is good.* [17] *As it is, it is no longer I myself who do it, but it is sin living in me.* [18] *For I know that good itself does not dwell in me, that is, in my sinful nature. For I have the desire to do what is good, but I cannot carry it out.* [19] *For I do not do the good I want to do, but the evil I do not want to do—this I keep on doing.* [20] *Now if I do what I do not want to do,*

it is no longer I who do it, but it is sin living in me that does it. ^{21} So I find this law at work: Although I want to do good, evil is right there with me. ^{22} For in my inner being I delight in God's law; ^{23} but I see another law at work in me, waging war against the law of my mind and making me a prisoner of the law of sin at work within me. ^{24} What a wretched man I am! Who will rescue me from this body that is subject to death?

Romans 7:15-24 (NIV)

Tim,

I found out that you have a whole part of you that I knew nothing about. I admit I am angry about all the times that I have questioned my value as a woman and all along it wasn't me. To think about the guilt you must have felt and the shame you lived with makes my heart sick. It makes me ache and want to turn back time and deal with this many years ago. I have so many questions I want to ask you, so many details I want to know. So many things make sense now, so many things that never seemed to "fit" before.

Mostly I wanted to say that I love you. I love you more today than I ever have. I feel closer to you today than I ever thought I could feel. But I am afraid that this feeling will go away, too. I am afraid that this closeness to you I am feeling is not shared by you. I am afraid that it is just a facade.

Do you feel closer to me? Are we really in a new place in our relationship? I need to know. I fear the feelings I have felt for you these many years have been one sided. I need to know that we are in the same place.

Thank you for being open with me.

Lately, when I look at you I want to be close to you so badly. But then I wonder if you are having sex with me now because you want to or because you are feeling guilty about the past. Your honesty caused me more pain than I ever thought possible. But because of that pain, because of your honesty, I have hope. I have hope that the kind of love I always dreamt about is out there for me, with you. The love that holds nothing back. The look in your eye that says I am it, only me. And until now I have never felt that. I have always known that there was another. I wasn't sure who she was. But, I pray with ALL my heart that she is out of your life. I pray that what I see is really there, not just a figment of my imagination.

Keep talking to me. Tell me everything you feel you can. I want to know everything about you. I have wasted so much time not fully knowing you. But I love you, probably too much for my own good.

Always yours,
Tina

P.S. I am not afraid of the truth—the truth will set us free.

Counselor's Corner:

Tina's explanation of fantasy is so true. When real life becomes too hard, our survival brain looks for ways to medicate and get rid of the stress. When porn is introduced early in life it becomes particularly difficult to deal with. The teen brain is being prepared for adulthood; in the process, huge pathways are being constructed that will indicate what brings pleasure and how to avoid pain. The internet makes this even more problematic because the internet reinforces the natural instinct for male brains. The hunt and pursuit and intrigue are all a part of the internet lure that appeals to the male brain.

As Dr. Roberts often says it is difficult for women to understand how a man can say he loves his wife and is also visiting porn sites. Men's brains can more easily compartmentalize their life because they have 40% less connections between the right and left side of the brain compared to women. He further states that we as women have the "upgraded" brain. We usually are better at integrating our emotional, sexual, and relational life. (*Betrayal & Beyond Book 1* that explains how the male brain is easily hijacked at an early age.)

Tina's struggle with trying to discern whether Tim was trustworthy when he first confessed is a struggle all women have. In fact, many husbands become angry and use a wife's Christian faith to divert the blame to her and deflect his behavior by stating, "As a Christian you are supposed to forgive and trust me." The truth is, forgiveness is a process and trust is earned.

The following excerpt is included in the *7 Pillars of Freedom Men's Workbook* to help a man understand what is required for him to gain trust from his wife. You may find this information helpful.

A woman's number one priority is safety, especially if there has been betrayal and trauma in her life. As pointed out in chapter 16 of the Pure Desire book, "Some women feel so violated they don't know if they even love their husbands anymore, let alone trust them. This is a normal response. There is a numbness that develops for her own self-protection. She doesn't want to be hurt again."[13]

Three Action Steps. For a woman's heart toward her husband to change, she needs to see three actions steps. Then and only then will she begin to trust him and feel safe.

The first action step is SINCERITY. A sincere heart is not only repentant, but is also willing to walk in behaviors that show sincerity. Notice in Proverbs 4: 23-27, there are action steps with outward evidence of guarding your heart, mouth, eyes and feet.

Keep vigilant watch over your heart; that's where life starts.

Don't talk out of both sides of your mouth; avoid careless banter, white lies, and gossip.

Keep your eyes straight ahead; ignore all sideshow distractions.

Watch your step, and the road will stretch out smooth before you.

Look neither right nor left; leave evil in the dust.

Your wife needs to see these actions being practiced daily. Again, she is the one that defines what it will take to regain trust. Some of your action steps might be participation in a Pure Desire group, checking in with your sponsor daily, getting professional counseling if needed, being proactive with recovery practices. Evidences that you are changing and are truly in recovery may include:

- *Fewer outbursts of anger*
- *Less demanding or controlling behavior*
- *Consistency in what is said and done*
- *Dependability and accountability (with time, finances, etc.)*

As she sees these outward behaviors, which are hopefully motivated from the inside out, trust begins to be restored.

The second action step is ABILITY. *The question that arises in her mind is, "He seems sincere and is trying, but does he have the ability to follow through and continue to grow?" Her greatest fear is that although the commitments seem sincere, in one year will he still be growing and moving toward health? Will he allow the Holy Spirit to help him move into new healing areas and is he willing to face whatever the issues are that drive his addiction?*

*The third action step is **DURABILITY**. She needs to know you are not doing these things to placate her now, and then later down the road go back to old habit patterns. Dr. Patrick Carnes has studied sexual addicts for years and has determined it takes 2 to 5 years for substantial healing and change to take place*[14]

In watching Ted go through these action steps, my trust and respect for him has grown through the years. He realized many years ago that his father wound was the main issue driving his addictions. He has allowed the Holy Spirit to walk with him, guide him, give him revelation and then make changes that are manifested in his outward behavior.

How are you doing in these three areas? Remember that we are not talking so much about performance as we are an attitude of the heart—what is in the heart is being worked out and shows in the behavior. [15]

As you can see from the statements I wrote in the *Seven Pillars* book for men, once Ted admitted to his struggle it was important for me to see him being proactive in getting help. Unfortunately, in the 1970's when he started his healing journey there was no Christian help available. That is what provoked him to find tools and write the book *Pure Desire*.

- ❤ *Journal what new information you learned about sexual addiction in this chapter that might help you to believe the addiction is not about you.*

- ❤ *Journal what might help you begin to have hope that your husband is starting his own healing journey.*

Chapter 4
Drip Torture

From my journals:

Lord, my heart aches so bad I can hardly stand it. Tim doesn't see why it would all bother me. I can't eat, I have trouble falling asleep, and I have lost all patience. I need you, Lord. I can't do this. I am so cold all of the time. Help me, Lord.

Due to the length of Tim's scheduled travel, we had planned for the girls and I to go to California to live with Tim for the summer, but because I felt it would be too disruptive on the girls, I was postponing it as long as possible. The counselor that we consulted within days of my finding out about Tim's addiction had said that, according to the Bible, it is not good for man to be alone; he recommended that the girls and I go to California as soon as possible to be with Tim. So the next week we left our home in the care of friends, as well as our pets, and boarded a flight to California.

I felt like I was in such a fog; I was going through the motions of the day but I didn't feel much of anything. I was determined to become whatever it was that Tim wanted in a woman, so I found myself watching to see where his eyes went when we were out together. I found myself hiding in pharmacies looking at men's magazines any chance I got—just to see what men wanted; then I worked to become what I saw. I started getting up every morning at 4:30 am to exercise before the kids got up, and I watched what I ate so obsessively that I eventually lost 30 pounds. I slathered my body with cellulite cream, anti-wrinkle cream, and self-tanning cream. I wanted so badly to become perfect so he wouldn't have any desire to look anywhere else.

In desperation I made a phone call to speak to someone, anyone who could tell me how to survive this pain. (1-800-New-Life and puredesire.org are great resources that can help change your life.) I realized I not only needed help for my marriage but also for my sanity. Doug, the therapist I found, listened to my story and was not in the least bit surprised. He told me the first thing I had to realize was that it was not about me. My husband's addiction had nothing to do with what I looked like or how I performed, and that I should try to get Tim to a workshop New Life Ministries called Every Man's Battle. I said Tim would never go. Besides, I told him, "Tim doesn't have an addiction to pornography, he just sometimes watches movies in the hotel when he travels." Doug snickered (this made me so angry) and asked what Tim did for a living. When I told him that Tim worked with computers, he told me there was most definitely porn involved. I disagreed and got off the phone, happy that my husband wasn't the "typical" man. Tim had told me he watched movies when he was away but when he was home he said he only brought up the old images in his mind. There was no porn on our computer, stated Tim, nor had there ever been. His biggest problem was the images that he "took" in his mind of women throughout his day.

When Tim got home that night I told him about the phone call I had made to New Life. Then I relayed the information about the workshop and told him what the counselor had said about the porn. He said *no* to the workshop; he didn't feel he needed it and he didn't have the time or the money. He also said that there wasn't any porn on our computer; he had already told me that. "Why would you ask again? Don't you trust me?" I said I did trust him, but inside I wondered if he was still lying. I wanted more than anything to believe him, but everything in me told me he was not being honest, and if he was not being honest about this, what else was he lying about? I wanted to know the truth, I needed to know the truth. I couldn't live with finding out a little at a time.

I continued to work out every morning and spent a lot of time alone in my room. I snooped through anything of Tim's that I thought would give me proof of the porn, never expecting to find anything. Then one day, at the very bottom of his suitcase, I found a hotel receipt. It was for several movies, one each night he was at the hotel. When I saw the money he had spent on them I felt sick; when I thought about all the time he had spent in hotels this past year alone, I became furious! He said he watched them every once in a while but this was several every night and these movies were expensive! I had never thought about the money. I never thought about the fact that this "stuff" took money away from our family!

Thoughts from my journal:

I feel like I am in a bad dream! I just want to wake up! When, Lord? When will he tell me the truth? God, I need the truth! Please!

I am angry every time I look at him. I feel like our relationship is so shallow.

I continued to talk to Doug almost every day. He was so patient with me. "It's not about you" was said almost every time we talked, but I just couldn't grasp how it could not be about me. I bought new clothes and started to like the way I looked. I no longer dressed motherly; I dressed to get attention. Men started to notice me and I started to think about having an affair. I'm not sure if it was to get back at Tim and let him see how it felt, or if it was to make myself feel desirable. I found myself making eye contact with men, especially if they were with younger women that I thought Tim would be attracted to.

I told Doug about this and he cautioned me to be *very* careful. He pointed out that I could not control what Tim did, but I could control what I did. "Guard your heart," he told me. He also continued to tell me about Every Man's Battle. I was convinced that Tim needed to go and I told him so. I would get off the phone with Doug and tell Tim, "Doug said there is porn," or "Doug said you need to go to EMB." Doug had become my hero, I needed him, and he was my link to reality.

After much badgering from me, Tim admitted that he did look at porn on our computer. "But just once or twice a month," he told me. I thought I would be so happy to find out the truth, but I was devastated. He looked at it in my home, on our computer? The one my kids used? He had lied straight to my face about it. How could I be such a fool to believe him and how could I still not tell when he was lying!

Thoughts from my journal:

I feel dead. Just nothing inside. The fact that he could look me straight in the eye and say there was no porn. He swore it and I couldn't see any sign of a lie. My entire life with him is a lie. What else don't I know? Not just about this. But what else don't I know?

I just want to go huddle in a corner and cry. I can never compete with his porn. I know I'm not supposed to. It's not about me! It's not about me! It's not about me!

My only hope was the workshop. If I could get him to the New Life workshop I knew everything would be okay. I decided to fast and pray. I wouldn't eat until Tim told me he would go to the Every Man's Battle workshop, and I would pray, somehow thinking that I needed to prove to God that this was important and that Tim needed to go. Or maybe I would get very sick and Tim would go just to make me start eating. (Either way this was unhealthy.) The next day Tim came to me and said, "I talked to that Doug guy at New Life and I signed up for that workshop. Are you happy now?" Yes, I was, but I was also afraid. *What if it didn't work? What if Doug was wrong? What if they just wanted our money?* It was quite an investment, and if it didn't work Tim would blame me for it. I called my new friend Doug and he said to trust him, it was truly worth it. He did, however, say that the recovery was up to Tim. I asked Doug a question that would haunt me for the next few years. "Is there anyone you know who made it to the other side of this? Is there any man who has gone to this workshop and never looked at porn or acted out again?" What I was asking for was an assurance that I would never have to feel this pain again, but Doug couldn't give it to me. He couldn't tell me of anyone he could point me to who now lived on the other side of this pain. I told him that if we survived and made it out of this mess, I would be a voice. I would scream from rooftops if I had to and tell women that it wasn't about them. I would tell them they are not alone. Little did I know what God had planned for me.

God can do anything...far more than you could ever imagine or guess or request in your wildest dreams."
Ephesians 3:20

Thoughts from my journal:

I just want the pain to stop.

Tell me one person who has made it through this. One person whose husband walked away from porn and never went back. Just one!

While my husband was away at the Every Man's Battle workshop I was very nervous. I had no idea what to expect when he got home and I was so afraid that nothing would change. I wanted so desperately to know that everything would be okay, that when he came home he would tell me how wrong he had been, and that he would never go back to the secrets and the lies. It was like going to the doctor to get a tumor removed; you are afraid that something will go wrong, yet you are excited that something is being done. You want to believe that once the treatment is completed you will be healed, but you don't want to get your hopes up for fear of being hurt even more. But please know that, as Doug told me, "It is not about you." There is nothing that you could have done. Nothing you could have worn. No way you could have looked. IT'S NOT ABOUT YOU!!!!! Any more than if your husband were addicted to drugs or alcohol. And it's not about sex, any more than alcoholism is about the alcohol. Stephen Arterburn puts it so well in his book *When You Love Too Much:* "Many wives believe that if they treat their husbands better, or have intercourse with them more regularly, the husband's addictive drives will be satisfied. This is like expecting an alcoholic to be satisfied by drinking more water. It doesn't work. The alcoholic's problem is not thirst; it is not solved merely by drinking liquid. Rather, it is alcohol that both fuels and satisfies the compulsion to numb and drown out pain."[16]

I have since learned from Pure Desire material that the same can be said for sexual addiction that starts out as a moral problem but quickly moves to a brain problem and becomes compulsive. Sexual addiction, like alcohol and drug addictions, changes the structure of the brain. The only way to heal any of these addictions is to go through detox and a program of genuine accountability. In the case of sexual addiction it is a two to five year process with a miracle every day. When healing steps are taken consistently over time, the brain can be changed.

Please also know that just because your husband has a sex addiction doesn't mean he is a horrible person. It means he has wounds from his past that he has learned to medicate with an addiction. Period. He is still a good person. I seemed to lose sight of this with Tim. Looking back I can see how patient he was during this time. I was so focused on my pain that I didn't notice him. I didn't notice how many times he would do the things that I normally did, like laundry or making dinner. I didn't notice the little gifts he would bring me. Looking back now, I can see that in his own way he was trying to make up for what he had done, and that he was in pain, too. He was watching me cry. He was watching me change into a shell of myself and he didn't know what to do about it. Some days he would tell me to "snap out of it" and other days he would cry and say he was sorry. He was just as confused as I was. He didn't know why he felt compelled to act out, and, as he said in the park that day, "Like I've prayed so many times before." He wanted to stop but he didn't have the necessary tools to know how to make a lasting change. The Every Man's Battle workshop helped him to see his need for other men's support in this battle and gain some tools towards healing.

The following Scripture points out that we are easy preys of temptation: "Watch and pray so that you will not fall into temptation. The spirit is willing but the flesh is weak" (Matthew 26:41). Without a battle plan and other men to join in the battle, the flesh will always win.

I want to caution you here. Many good intentioned people (especially in the church) who don't understand sexual addiction will try to "help" you figure out "why" it happened. Quite often this means pointing out what you could have done differently. Do not allow yourself to take the blame. Remember again, it's not about you. I also want to caution you not to allow others to trivialize it. Yes, many men look at porn, and yes, society has made it acceptable, but Scripture challenges us when we come to Christ to no longer walk as the world:

And so I insist—and God backs me up on this—that there be no going along with the crowd, the empty-headed, mindless crowd. They've refused for so long to deal with God that they've lost touch not only with God but with reality itself. They can't think straight anymore.

Feeling no pain, they let themselves go in sexual obsession, addicted to every sort of perversion. But that's no life for you. You learned Christ! My assumption is that you have paid careful attention to him, been well instructed in the truth precisely as we have it in Jesus. Since, then, we do not have the excuse of ignorance, everything—and I do mean everything— connected with that old way of life has to go. It's rotten through and through. Get rid of it! And then take on an entirely new way of life—a God-fashioned life, a life renewed from the inside and working itself into your conduct as God accurately reproduces his character in you. (Ephesians 4:17-24 The Message)

Ephesians goes on to say to be renewed in the spirit of your mind. An addict's mind has been hijacked by this world; when the addict gets Biblical tools and the support of other men, he can find healing.

For your personal healing, it is important to mourn the loss. When you find out about your husband's addiction something dies inside of you. You thought you were living life one way, only to find out things were not as they seem. It may sometimes feel like a giant rug has been pulled out from beneath your feet and your whole life is suspended in the air. You stand there, helpless, wondering where the pieces of your life are going to land and you wonder what shape they will be in when they hit the ground. But our God has large hands. And if you ask Him to help you He will catch the many pieces of your life and place them gently where He wants them to be. And years later you will be able to look back and see that your life has ended up right where it needed to be.

The best advice that I can give you right now is do not be afraid and be strong. You are beginning a very painful journey and you will need help. I am going to share with you the Scriptures that I found the most helpful during this time. Some of them might be very familiar, but if you look at them with new eyes and draw new meaning and strength from them they may help you greatly.

Psalm 23 (NIV). *The LORD is my shepherd, I lack nothing. He makes me lie down in green pastures, he leads me beside quiet waters, he refreshes my soul. He guides me along the right paths for his name's sake. Even though I walk through the darkest valley, I will fear no evil, for you are with me; your rod and your staff, they comfort me. You prepare a table before me in the presence of my enemies. You anoint my head with oil; my cup overflows. Surely your goodness and love will follow me all the days of my life, and I will dwell in the house of the LORD forever.*

Psalm 23 helped me to know that no matter where I was or what I was feeling, God saw me. He knew where I was, and even though I was overwhelmed and didn't know where to turn, He was there guiding me. I didn't have to think, I didn't have to *do* anything. If I let Him, if I followed Him like a sheep, trusting Him, He would guide me and protect me, no matter what. He loved me and would comfort me.

Psalm 27:1 (NIV). *The LORD is my light and my salvation—whom shall I fear? The LORD is the stronghold of my life—of whom shall I be afraid?*

Psalm 91:4 (NASB). *He will cover you with His pinions, and under His wings you will find refuge....*

Deuteronomy 33:27 (NLT). *The eternal God is your refuge, and his everlasting arms are under you. He drives out the enemy before you; he cries out, 'Destroy them!' Destroy!*

I love these three verses because they promise you that God is right there with you. You are not alone. I am comforted by the imagery of a mother bird protecting her babies from harm, covering their ears and their eyes from seeing or hearing bad things. God does not want you to go and look for/at the porn to see what it is that attracts your husband. It doesn't matter. It is all a fantasy and it does not reflect on you. Like a mother bird, God does not want you to be exposed to that "stuff" anymore than he wanted your husband exposed to it.

Matthew 18:15-17 (NIV). *If your brother sins against you go and show him his fault, just between the two of you. If he listens to you, you have won your brother over. But if he will not listen, take one or two others along, so that "every matter may be established by the testimony of two or three witnesses."*

When you find out about your husband's addiction he may deny it at first, or he may say that it is none of your business. He may get angry and defensive and may even try to blame you for his actions. But you must confront him if things are ever going to change. As terrible as it may be to confront him, most men actually want to be caught, they are so tired of living with this secret and they want help. Your husband more than likely knows what he is doing is wrong, and he has probably tried many times to overcome it; the problem is, he doesn't know how. Your confrontation may be just what he needs to start to heal. Don't be afraid. God will help you to do this, as He promises.

Joshua 1:5-6 (NKJ). *… I will be with you. I will not leave you nor forsake you. Be strong and of good courage….*

Joshua 1:9 (NASB). *Have I not commanded you? Be strong, and courageous! Do not tremble or be dismayed, for the Lord your God is with you wherever you go.*

Deuteronomy 31:6 (NASB). *Be strong and courageous, do not be afraid or tremble at them, for the Lord your God is the one who goes with you. He will not fail you or forsake you.*

2 Timothy 1:7(NIV). *For the Spirit God gave us does not make us timid, but gives us power, love and self-discipline.*

In the Pure Desire support group for women that I am presently leading, I am seeing women rise up and find their voices, not in a disrespectful way, but in a caring and assertive way. The group support has helped individual women to not shrink back, but to love their husband enough to speak the truth in love.

Some people may tell you that it is not godly to be angry. They say to forgive and move on. Yes, there is a place for that, and if you are there right now, good for you. But I wasn't. I hated Tim. God leaves room for these feelings. Listen to the pain and anger that God felt towards Israel:

When Israel was only a child, I loved him. I called out, 'My son!' ---called him out of Egypt. But when others called him, he ran off and left me. He worshiped the popular sex gods, he played at religion with toy gods,. Still, I stuck with him. I led Ephraim. I rescued him from human bondage, but he never acknowledged my help, never admitted that I was the one pulling the wagon, That I lifted him, like a baby, to my cheek, that I bent down to free him. Now he wants to go back to Egypt or go over to Assyria--- anything but return to me! ...But how can I give up on you....How can I turn you loose...How can I leave you to be ruined like Admah, devastated like luckless Zeboim? I can't bear to even think such thoughts. My insides churn in protest. And so I'm not going to act on my anger. I'm not going to destroy Ephraim. And why? Because I am God and not a human. I'm The Holy One and I'm here—in your very midst.

Hosea 11:1-4, 8-9 (The Message)

Can't you just feel his sadness and anger, the same sadness that you and I feel? We look at this man we love so much who has hurt us so badly and we have such a mixture of emotions. We can't believe that he could do something so vial against us and we ache. We want to remind him how much we love him and the sacrifices that we have made for him, and yet we want to destroy him and make him pay. God knows how you are feeling. He has been there. And He will be there for you. Trust Him, and ask Him to help you.

Psalm 16:1-2 (NIV). *Keep me safe, my God, for in you I take refuge. I say to the LORD, "You are my Lord; apart from you I have no good thing."*

I needed to trust God to protect me. Since I couldn't trust Tim, I needed to lean on God. Know that God will not let you down. He is a safe place to hide, and cry, and tell all your fears. He will not judge you no matter what you say, and He will never stop loving you.

Psalm 27:7 (NIV). *Hear my voice when I call, LORD; be merciful to me and answer me.*

Sometimes we may feel like God doesn't hear us when we cry out to him. Sometimes we just want to shout, "Hear me!" and "Answer me!" God understands.

There were days when just to get out of bed seemed too difficult. I remember telling the kids that I was sick. And I really did feel sick. I was weak and tired and overwhelmed. Again, God understands. Cry out to Him. The Psalmist did.

Psalm 31:9 (NKJ). *Have mercy on me, O LORD, for I am in trouble; my eye wastes away with grief, yes, my soul and my body.*

When Tim went to the Every Man's Battle workshop, I was worried that it "wouldn't work" or that I would do something to mess up Tim's progress or undo what New Life had done. But the truth is that if your husband is not truly broken or repentant, chances are he will be stuck in his sexual sin. His healing and recovery are between him and God. It is his battle to face and work on, and if he chooses to stay in that place of sin it is his choice.

Recently I asked Tim if there was anything I could have done during that time to hinder his recovery. He responded that at times when I was very angry and non-forgiving towards him, he would think, *What is the use of trying so hard? It doesn't make a difference. She will never trust me.* But then he would realize it wasn't about anything that I did or didn't do, it was up to him. I have found that many men feel a bit of "entitlement factor." They minimize the sin because they believe they are overworked and underappreciated; therefore, looking at porn and masturbating is no big deal. Although on a much smaller scale, it's kind of like when I eat something I probably shouldn't because I "had a bad day."

The important thing is to get him to Every Man's Battle or a Pure Desire group for men. Let them and God do the rest.

Counselor's Corner

You, like Tina, might want someone like Doug to assure you that there is a quick fix that will keep your spouse from acting out and never going back to this behavior. No one can guarantee that. But having worked with couples for over 25 years in Pure Desire Ministries helping them to find victory in this area, I can say there are thousands who are walking in real freedom. What has been the key? First, as Tina pointed out, the husband has to be willing to do whatever it will take to get healing. Real healing. Sadly, most churches want him to just Try Harder—which never works—and is why many men have given up.

Tina didn't give up, she kept pressing the issue; that is the key role of the wife—to set healthy boundaries, to have a Safety Action Plan and possibly ask him to take a polygraph test every three to six months. A shortened example of a Safety Action Plan and guidelines for polygraph tests are included in the resource section of this book; the Safety Action Plan is explained in detail in *Betrayal & beyond Book* 2. The polygraph not only helps her to know the bottom line, especially if she is at risk for STDs and or HIV, but also it helps him to know that there will be an objective way of knowing if he is lying. Lying is part of the addiction that has been in his life since early teens. If he chooses real healing, this process will help him to get honest with others, but more than that, honest with himself.

You might ask, "Diane, how can I know he won't relapse?" As he starts the process he may relapse, but within thirty to ninety days, if he is engaged in the process of healing, the sexual activity should stop. It is then up to him to decide, with the tools he gets through Pure Desire Ministries, if he is going to make this a new lifestyle of freedom.

Dr. Ted Roberts likens the process to when he had fractured his foot when running. He went to a specialist who fitted him with new running shoes, gave him some strengthening exercises, and showed him how to run in a new way. The specialist said if he incorporated these principles into his life, he would be able to run in new freedom.

Men caught in sexual bondage have a fracture in their soul. With the biblical and clinical tools and group support that are offered through Pure Desire Ministries, men learn a new lifestyle. They can learn to live free of their addiction and walk in honesty and intimacy with their wife. It is hard work; it requires the renewing of the mind and true accountability where the husband is taught to use tools that will keep him in a place of restoration and health.

I tell women that if he is doing nothing for his own personal healing, he is planning relapse. The enemy knows the fracture in his soul and if the husband chooses to be passive, the enemy will overtake him.

Tina's struggle to want to control Tim's healing process is one all women struggle with. That is why it is so important for wives to be involved in a Betrayal & Beyond group. (Or if there is not a group in your area, get Betrayal & Beyond Book 2, which explains the safety plan and polygraph.) Understanding healthy boundaries and having a safety plan that reinforces those healthy boundaries will keep the wife from being a victim and feeling helpless.

Finally, Tina's admonition to trust God is essential. I say two things to women. One is that if a man has a heart for God, he doesn't stand a chance of staying stuck in his addiction with a praying wife! God's ear is always open to her crying out to Him on her husband's behalf.

Two, there are no quick fixes. Chances are the husband has been using sex to medicate his pain for 10, 20, 30 plus years. God will not pull out his brain and give him a new one. In Romans 12:2 Paul admonishes us to not be conformed to this world, but be transformed by the renewing of your mind. When we come to Christ, He renews our spirit (we are born again). But it takes work and partnership with God and others to create a new lifestyle designed to reprogram his brain.

❤ *Journal your fears about letting go and trusting a healing process.*

❤ *Journal a prayer for your husband to start the healing journey. Or, if he has started, write a payer that includes some specific things you sense you need to pray over him.*

Peace Beyond the Tears

Chapter 5
His Box of Junk Revealed

Thoughts from my journals:

I vacillate between hating Tim so much to loving him so much. I want to run away. I want to get away from all this thinking so badly!

I hate sex! The very idea makes me angry!

I don't want to wear my wedding ring anymore.

The Friday Tim left for his Every Man's workshop was one of the most apprehensive days of my life. I had so much riding on this. What if it didn't work? I needed so badly for it to work. He called me that night in tears saying he was so sorry for everything he had done. He was sorry for his addiction and he was sorry for all the years that he had kept me emotionally at a distance. He also said he had learned some things about himself and what drove him towards his addiction. I was pleased with his phone call but not sure if I believed his words. Saturday flew by, and then came Sunday. I was so worried about him coming home. I was afraid that I would do something to mess up whatever New Life had done for him. When he got home I met him at the car, I didn't want the kids to get to him first. He stepped out of the car and held me so tight while he cried. He told me they had told him to disclose everything when he got home, but that he needed me to be patient with him until he was ready to tell me. Let me say here that there are some people who think that full disclosure is too overwhelming for the wives, but I disagree. Before Tim went to the workshop I got the drip torture; every day there seemed to be a new small confession from his past, or I would come up with another question or more doubts. I found myself screaming inside, waiting for the Big One—that one piece of information that would shatter my world completely. And now, here I was, on the brink of finding out. I felt I couldn't breathe, but I agreed to be patient.

The next few days were excruciating. What more did he have to tell me? I was sick to my stomach. I couldn't eat, I couldn't concentrate, and I felt like I was going to explode. I hated myself that he had this much power over me! What gave him the right to tell me that he had more to say and then not say it? I thought he was just being controlling and manipulative.

Finally the day came when he had worked up the courage to disclose everything, but he asked me not to say a word until he was done. He told me he acted out much more than he had told me he did, he told me of some things that happened in his past that he believes led him to his addiction, he told me that he acted out when he was stressed, insecure, or lonely, and he told me that he never felt accepted by his father and that acting out sometimes made him feel accepted and powerful. But then he told me that every time he acted out he hated himself and in the end he felt more lonely and isolated. He felt like more of a failure because he couldn't control himself. One of the saddest things he told me was that he would celebrate going a day without acting out. Then he would challenge himself to go two then three days. He said that one time he actually made it to a month without acting out, and how proud of himself he had been. But his victory was short lived as the computer beckoned or some sexy image would pass by him.

I sat there listening. I didn't know what to say or do. I was sad, angry, and hurt. I felt betrayed and confused and then guilty. *How could I not know? Where was I when he was struggling? If he wanted sex why didn't he just come to me?*

How could I not see his pain all these years? How could he do this to me?

Tim told me that at the Every Man's Battle workshop they told the men to be prepared to answer all of their wife's questions. They also told them to be prepared for their wife to be angry. Over the next few days I asked Tim many questions, which he patiently took the time to answer. I wanted to know everything I could, from web addresses to what exactly he took mental images of. I was obsessed to know every detail. The more I knew, the more I became angry. *The lady bending over to put her child in the stroller? Are you serious? The jogger in the park? Why? Lingerie catalogues? The ones I bought so you would notice me? You mentally had sex with them?????* *Adds on the computer? Websites? Images?* It was everywhere! From the park, to the store, to my home. I couldn't get away from them. His lover was everywhere I turned. I started watching where his eyes went when we were out together. *Did he look long enough to take a snapshot?* I started noticing pretty young girls everywhere I went. Billboards, posters, shopping centers. It was all too much! One day I was walking in Target with my kids and I looked up and saw a poster on the wall of a woman in a bra and panties. I started to cry in the store as my knees gave way beneath me at the thought that my husband would not have sex with me all these years because he had already had sex with "her" in his mind. Her and many others like her. I hated him so much! And I hated them, each and every one of them!

While Tim was relieved to have all this "stuff" off his chest, I was now weighed down with it. It was as though he came home with this big box of his junk and handed it to me. He was excited that he no longer had to carry it and was anxious to get to work on his "plan" and he couldn't understand why I was so overwhelmed and sad. While he was feeling so close to God and his family I was left feeling that my world was crashing in on me, my entire reality had been turned upside down. This man I thought I knew so well just told me how little I actually knew him.

Thoughts from my journals:

I feel like I just had major open-heart surgery. I am afraid I won't be okay. I am afraid that I won't heal properly and this will take a very long time. I know that, like surgery, I need to take one day at a time, but it is so hard not to look at the what-ifs. The surgery seems so unnecessary. Like Tim just elected to tear me open and now he is running around looking at other women as I am laid up in horrible pain.

I am so tired of being angry all the time!

The books I'm reading talk about the intense need for pleasure. And how, when they see a pretty girl they twinge and have the desire. And in their mind they are having their way with the girl. So…who was she? Was I with him when he saw her? Or is it some old memory keeping him company?

I can't wait until winter when everyone wears sweaters!

Tim was given a list of things to do to help him with his recovery: read the Bible, exercise, talk to another man (accountability partner), read recovery literature, take time for himself weekly, and get counseling. Tim called these things his "metrics" and each week he had to check in with a group he had joined at the Every Man's Battle workshop called Sustained Victory and report how he was doing with his metrics. He made a chart where he would check the boxes after he had completed each of his tasks; when he had made his phone call to his group each week, he would have to tell the other men in his group how he was doing with his metrics. I knew that Tim would not want to have to tell the other men that he had not been doing what he was supposed to do. This gave me comfort. He was pretty good at doing most of the things on his chart and it was such a comfort to see his chart full. As long as his chart was full I knew he wouldn't act out, at least that is what I convinced myself. I needed some proof that he was being honest with me; in the beginning, his chart and his weekly phone call were the only things I trusted.

As Tim worked his metrics he started to change; at first he became very sentimental. Without his addiction in the way, he began to see his family for the first time and I think he was realizing what we meant to him. He started reading a couple's devotional and praying with me every morning, he got angry less frequently and was less agitated. Proving himself at work became less of a priority, and he became patient and thoughtful. Then he began what he called "bouncing his eyes." If a woman walked by, Tim he would look the other way; if a women was dressed a bit inappropriately, Tim would avoid her like the plague. He would turn his head during movie scenes that he thought might show a woman in a risky situation. He worked hard to make sure that *nothing* compromised his thought life. I was proud of him. But (there always seems to be a but) I was angry, too, because I didn't understand why I wasn't enough for him. Why did he have to go to such extreme measures to guard his thought life? Was I really so undesirable that he had to force himself to look away from others. *It's not about you! It's not about you! It's not about you!* I loved the changes I was seeing in Tim. He was becoming the godly man I always thought he was, but change is hard, even if it is for the better.

As Tim was becoming closer to God, I seemed to be pulling away. He would come out to the living room early in the morning to do devotions and I would become angry because I normally exercised during this time, it was *my* time. (But he is reading his Bible!) I would make a mental note to wake up even earlier. When he would take time for himself and go fishing once a week, I would seethe, wondering when I was going to be able to take some time. Every time he would celebrate a victory or brag about how good he was doing, hate would creep up inside of me. He would meet with a men's group once a week and I would wonder when I was ever going to be able to get together with women. *He did this! He betrayed me! Why is it that he gets rewarded for doing what he should have done in the first place!*

I became resentful and bitter. I was short with my kids and mean to Tim. I ate too little and was not happy unless I was in pain from exercising. I was trying desperately to find the perfection that would keep Tim from "going back there." I felt forgotten and overlooked; everything seemed to revolve around him and his recovery. I started trying to be what I thought he wanted so badly; I would dress provocatively to get his attention, bend over seductively when I knew he was looking, and come onto him anytime we were alone. He didn't notice my attempts and still turned me down.

My friend Doug at New Life warned me to not to become Tim's replacement porn; he said that Tim was working on becoming intimate and that by reducing myself to something that I wasn't, I would only hinder the process. By becoming what he was trying to stop needing, Doug cautioned, I was allowing Tim to relate to me in a non-intimate way. Tim had to learn to allow his heart to be vulnerable with me, not just his body. He recommended that I just be myself, not try so hard, and let Tim come on to me. "Don't make it easy on him," Doug cautioned. And then Doug recommended that I go to a workshop called Every Heart Restored, a workshop New Life sponsored for women whose husbands were going through the battle.

Thoughts from my journals:

I'm not sure who I am anymore. I am trying to be attractive to Tim, but I am not sure how to be that.

He is working hard to heal, but none of it includes me.

I am not living. I am surviving, and hiding, and avoiding. I really feel lost.

I miss my kids and they are right here. I miss me. I miss my old simple problems. This one is just too big.

This was a very difficult time. In my opinion it is the worst time in all this mess they call recovery. I hated it. I wish I could go back to the "me" that I was and tell me I would make it through all this. I wish I could tell me that even though I felt forgotten by the rest of the world, God has not forgotten me and that he knows where I would be in a couple of years. The same for you; God has not forgotten you and He will see you through this.

"For I know the plans that I have for you," says the Lord. "They are plans for good and not for disaster, to give you a future and a hope." (Jeremiah 29:11 NLT)

When Tim came back from the Every Man's Battle workshop, he was on a mission. At the time I was angry and resentful. I got angry when he would look away or bounce his eyes. I got angry when he spent time away with other men or by himself. I was angry when he rewarded himself for good behavior or when he patted himself on the back. But now, looking back, I see that those things he was doing were really for my benefit. Him looking away wasn't because the women were more appealing than me, it was because he desired true intimacy with me and didn't want any other image to get in the way of that. He was honoring and respecting me, but at the time it was a clumsy effort that was very obvious and it hurt my feelings. As far as spending time away, he needed that in order to regroup. Disciplining his eyes was a very hard thing to do; disciplining his thought life was even harder. He needed a break from it and he needed to reward himself.

Think of it as though your husband is recovering from a serious illness. You didn't cause it, you can't cure it, and there is nothing that you can do other than pray for him and be there for him when he needs you. You have to keep yourself physically, emotionally, and spiritually healthy. Instead of getting resentful of the time he is taking, take some time for you, reward yourself and try to spend some time talking to other people. If you don't feel comfortable talking to others take more time to journal your reactions and emotions. It is amazing how healing it has been to go back and read all of my old journals and how wonderful it was when I was going through it to be able to write how angry I was or how much I hated Tim—all without being judged. You can always burn them later if you want to.

Please see the value in you and don't let your value be determined by what your husband is or is not doing. He is fighting a battle right now and probably can't see past his own inner struggles to see your pain. Romans 7:21-24 says, *"When I want to do good evil is right there."* Give him a little space; he will be doing quite a bit of thinking and, hopefully, will be working with other men using tools that will help his healing. He will need time and patience and understanding, even though this is the last thing you feel that he deserves. I promise you that in the end, the time he spends working on himself and getting closer to God will help him to be the man God always intended him to be much quicker. The husband you could have on the other end could be a man of integrity.

Thoughts from my journals:

Tim is my hero. He is facing his problems head on and he is truly trying to have the mind of Christ.

Looking back over the years of rejection, were they anything compared to what is happening to Tim now?

I am proud of how far Tim has come, but now I need to start working on me.

I know it will be hard, but try not to compare yourself to his pornography; the women in those pictures don't look like that either and even if you did look like that, it wouldn't matter. Like I've said before, what they look like is not what draws your husband to them; it goes way deeper than that. If you look at the women that you consider sexy and perfect in Hollywood, most of their spouses have cheated on them in one way or another, so it is not about looks. If you try to become what it is that you see in his porn, you cheapen you. You will begin to dislike yourself for what you have become and in the process you may start to try to get attention from other men. But think about their wives, do we really want to be the woman that their husband is dreaming about when she thinks he is making love to her? Ok, so maybe a part of us does, but God's Word is clear about not being a stumbling block. How much do we want to kill the women who were a stumbling block to our husbands? Do you really want to be "that woman?"

When Tim came back from Every Man's Battle and was willing to answer all of my questions, I asked him everything I could think of and he answered every question. Some questions I really wish I hadn't asked him, things that I really did not need to know and that caused me more heartache and grief. I caution you here to pray about the questions before you ask them. Knowing exactly what the girls looked like, their bra sizes, and what they did may just give you more things with which to compare yourself. Also, knowing the web addresses that he viewed may only cause you more curiosity; if you choose to look at these sites you are playing in the enemies' playground. Please know that there are many women who are addicted to pornography and it has to start somewhere.

You are wounded right now and you are looking for answers and affirmation. Please look to Christ and protect your heart. "For we do not wrestle against flesh and blood, but against principalities, against powers, against the rulers of the darkness of this age, against spiritual *hosts* of wickedness in the heavenly *places*" (Ephesians 6:12). Please be careful and cautious with your tender heart!

Tim,

I am very proud of you and the effort you are making. I continue to see such wonderful change in you. And every so often I think I can feel your heart reaching out to mine. It's like I peek into a window in heaven. I want so badly to climb into the window of the 'real, true Tim' and make you trust me. I want to feel all the love that I know is in there. But I know that I must be patient. I know that healing takes time.

Thank you for today. Thank you for spending time with me. I enjoyed it very much. You told me I was sexy. You made me feel beautiful today. You told me you watched me, and you told me I was sexy. You made me feel like the most beautiful woman in the world to you. I cannot tell you in words how much I desire to feel like that. I truly never thought I would.

So, as your healing takes place you are helping me to heal as well.

Thank you again for one of the most memorable and fulfilling and confident days of my life. Thank you for working to heal. And thank you for letting me 'peek' at your heart. I hope someday for you to open the door and ask me in.

I love you will all my heart.

Forever,

Tina

Counselor's Corner

Tina brought up some important issues that were part of her personal healing process, including disclosure and learning a new normal.

Disclosure

Tina shared how Tim, like many addicts, takes the "drip torture" approach to disclosure. Studies by Omar Minwalla show that when staggered disclosure takes place, the wife experiences symptoms much like someone with post-traumatic stress or a rape victim.[17] "Initially the man denies everything, then discloses what he thinks he can get away with, then a bit more and finally after he is confronted as more details come out, he discloses everything. This is the typical sequence that 58.7% of addicts follow and it is horrific for the spouse."[18]

The goal of full disclosure is to establish a basis to rebuild trust. For the husband, this makes his accountability real because everything is out on the table and the secrets no longer have any power over him. It also gives the wife ability to make healthy choices based on truth, even though initially she will feel like he has just dumped all his pain on her.

From my experiences in the counseling office, I know that every time disclosure has taken place, the wife goes through a painful rollercoaster of emotions even when I have helped prepare her for whatever her worst fears are. I do not recommend disclosure without the wife having a Betrayal & Beyond support group and/or a counselor to walk her through the revelation of her husband's secret life.

The ideal is that the husband would write a statement and read it to his group and or/counselor before sharing with his wife. He should also be prepared to answer her questions. But, as I caution women in Betrayal & Beyond Book 1, too much information will keep you stuck in you healing process. Details such as color of hair, measurements, what sexual activities your husband did with her, etc., will keep you stuck in comparison mode. Remember it is not about you; it is about how he is medicating his pain. Appropriate questions he should answer are:

- What was the time frame for each incident in which he acted out?

- What sexual activity did you engage in that did not involve physical acts, such as fantasy, flirting, planning to act out?

- How much money was spent?

- What health issues should I be aware of, including the possibility of STDs and HIV?

- Will I run into someone I know with whom you have been involved?

If the husband is coached properly (by his counselor or group), he will stick to sharing information without justifying his behavior.

Sadly, Tina had no group to help her immediately process her pain. It would have been helpful to have women validate the emotional ups and downs she was experiencing, such as deep sadness, anger, depression, heaviness, etc.

If the wife has no one to help her process, she can easily turn on the addict out of anger and shame him. Remember shame drives his addiction. That is why she needs help in processing her pain and he needs the support of a group or counselor after he shares with his wife so he doesn't slide into a shame cycle.

Learning a new normal

Tina could have been helped through this process had she

had a group and some information that would have shown her how her healing journey would be impacted by new healthy choices Tim was making in his life. The *Betrayal & Beyond* material helps the wife understand that her spouse's main focus for the first thirty to ninety days will be stopping the addictive behavior. Using tools and creating some healthy alternatives to his acting out are important.

In the past when stress came, Tim had trained his brain to immediately go to acting out to relieve the pain. His survival brain would kick in and he would automatically go to the place that would relieve stress—porn and masturbation. By doing things that nurtured him, Tim was trying to come up with new alternatives.

In Pure Desire we not only want addicts to have healthy alternatives, but we also want them to begin to engage their pre-frontal cortex. The lie most addicts believe (since age six when their survival brain was fully formed) is that whatever the stress, it is too overwhelming to face. As a six-year-old or even as a teen, that is true. Without a fully developed prefrontal cortex, which takes 25 years to develop, the cravings to relieve the pain will be overwhelming. The tools in *The Seven Pillars of Freedom* help men learn how to engage their prefrontal cortex and how to become aware when they are starting their ritual that automatically leads them to relapse. Once aware that they have started down the addictive path, they learn to identify the double bind: choose to relapse or choose to face the fear or stress they are medicating. We want them to face their pain rather than medicate it. With the tools provided and the encouragement of other men in their group, they can be victorious.

As Tim started making healthy choices, Tina, even though she hated his acting out, had learned how to do their tango from hell. In the new waltz from heaven she, too, was going to need to learn some new dance steps. Tina found herself in a double bind: keep doing the old dance where she knew the steps or learn a new dance routine that seemed scary and unfamiliar. Remember, intimacy isn't comfortable; it will challenge us to move out of our comfort zones to become uncomfortably close.

Journal

❤ *If you have experienced full or partial disclosure, journal your feelings.*

❤ *If full disclosure hasn't yet happened, journal your fears and emotions.*

❤ *In hearing Tina and Tim's story, what might be some fears you would face in regards to a "new normal"?*

Chapter 6
Reacting to Disclosure

Tim came home from Every Man's Battle beaten, which is right where God needed him to be. He was repentant and ready to do whatever it took to recover. He was also overwhelmed. He had been addicted to pornography since he was a teenager, which meant that he had been living with a secret lie all those years. He had resolved in the past never to "go there" again. He now knew he wasn't alone and had the tools to recover. "What if it doesn't work?" still lingered in his mind.

For anyone to honestly examine the secret sin in their life, the stuff they try to keep hidden, even from themself, had to be very difficult. Imagine having to look someone in the eyes and tell them that you masturbated to porn, and what kind, and when. Imagine having to tell her that you waited until she was in bed when you thought she would be asleep and you surfed the internet for someone to masturbate to, telling her how the thought of acting out sometimes started in the morning and you would try to keep the thoughts away; you even tried to pray them away. How you tried to stay busy throughout the day just so you wouldn't think about it, how by the middle of the day the compulsion was so strong you could think of nothing else, and by the end of the day you didn't care what the cost, you had to have your "fix." And then to tell her that you would wait for the right time, when she and the kids were in bed asleep, to go and get your "hit," and afterwards, you felt so lonely and guilty. Afterwards you hated yourself for being so stupid and you would vow NEVER to do it again.

For Tim to come home and disclose everything, to tell the woman he loved most in the world, all his deep dark secrets must have terrified him. What if I hated him? What if I completely rejected him and left with the kids. He was already feeling completely humbled and vulnerable. He must have felt scared about the possibility of losing the kids and me. Remember, one of the reasons they "go there" is fear of rejection; so when he came home and didn't tell me everything right away, he wasn't being mean and controlling like I thought he was, he was just trying to process everything enough to tell me. If this is your husband, please be patient, especially if he is with a group of men who understand sexual addiction and are encouraging him. Give him time. When he does open up and disclose the truth and the full extent of his addiction ask questions, keeping in mind the guidelines for questions presented in the Counselor's Corner at the end of the previous chapter. I encourage you to have a counselor and/or a group of women supporting you through this process.

After Tim disclosed everything, I felt very guilty and wondered how I could not have known that he was in the midst of this battle. Please try to resist feeling guilty. Most addicts become very good at lying, keeping secrets and making their wives feel crazy.

When I saw the billboards and the posters of scantily clad young women, I hated those girls! I even found myself resenting the sexuality of my teenage daughters because I couldn't compete no matter how much weight I lost or what I did to my skin. We are not meant to compete, and our husbands don't want us to. God doesn't want us to compete, either; He wants us to draw near to Him during this time. Now is the time to find out who we are in Christ, apart from our husbands. Then, if they do fall, we will be able to continue standing.

When I mentioned that I started to dress to get attention

and that Doug cautioned me to be *very* careful, I was in a very dangerous place where I could have easily fallen prey to a sexual addiction because my spirit was weak and I was very vulnerable. Think of the damage I would have caused if I had followed through with my desire to get back at Tim by having an affair; think of the example I would have been to my girls. We need to be strong, and we can't do it on our own which is why we have other women helping us to heed the warning in Colossians 4:2, "Devote yourselves to prayer, being watchful and thankful."

I pray over you the same prayer the Apostle Paul prayed over Christians in the early church: May God "…fill you with the knowledge of His will through all the wisdom and understanding that the Spirit gives" (Colossians 1:9 NIV). Paul also reminds Christians to "…set your hearts on things above, where Christ is seated at the right hand of God. Set your minds on things above, not on earthly things" (Colossians 3:1-2 NIV).

Satan loves it when we think that we can recover on our own. But it is a lie. Your husband will need help to recover from his sexual addiction. The first step he has to take is to admit that he has a struggle with porn. He must admit it to himself and admit it to you. If your husband does not believe that he has a problem, any amount of treatment he receives won't help. (By the way, viewing pornography is nearly always accompanied by masturbation.)

Next, your husband should seek some real accountability. He must find a group of men who understand sexual addiction and he must be willing to be honest and have true accountability. Most accountability groups are binge and purge groups where each week people reports how they did during the week; if they mess up, the message from the group is, "Don't do it again." This is a "try harder" approach—and it does not bring lasting change.

Pure Desire group leaders are trained to help addicts

problem-solve and immediately make changes that can move them back to a place of health and restoration. In addition to keeping a check on where men are on that slippery slope to relapse, men are also challenged to share how they are doing on what they had committed to change the previous week. Each week the men are challenged with questions similar to these:

- How did you do on your commitment to change last week?

- Have you lied to anyone this week directly or indirectly?

- What area do you need to work on this week for change to occur in your life?

- What will it cost you if you don't change?

- What fears will you need to face in order to make these changes?

- Who are you willing to call at least three times this week so they can hold you accountable for the changes you are committed to making tonight?

The more your husband knows about addiction the less power it will have on him. If he knows his triggers he can try to fight them off. He can call his accountability partner and use positive affirmations that declare who God says he is, such as, "I am a conqueror in Christ and I can have the mind of Christ." (Romans 12:2 is one of my husband's favorite scriptures. "Do not conform to the pattern of this world, but be transformed by the renewing of your mind. Then you will be able to test and approve what God's will is—his good, pleasing and perfect will.") He can also remind himself why he is making these changes—for himself, his wife, and his children.

Sometimes a period of sexual abstinence is recommended if pornographic images come to mind during sex. The idea is to starve the pornographic imagination of the drugs he has become accustomed to. (But don't tell him I said that) Sexual abstinence can also be a way of helping him to face the pain he has been medicating. He needs to realize he can stand in the midst of pain and let the feelings and fears of the past sweep over him without running to his addiction. Also, with the tools he gains from the group he can problem solve rather than numb out to avoid living in the present.

He should find healthy ways for his body to produce the endorphins and adrenaline to which he has become addicted. Strenuous exercise, competitive sports, and mental exercises are all good ways for the body to produce these chemicals. And they will build self-confidence.

Looking back, I wish I would have known how much Tim loved me and I wish I could have seen how scared he was. I wish I could have looked at his struggles as an addiction, not as a betrayal. But I don't know if that is possible when a woman is in the initial phases of discovery about her husband's addiction, when she is probably too hurt and confused and scared herself. I also wish that I would have let it be Tim's battle and not taken it upon myself to be his gatekeeper who watched everything that he looked at and drowned myself with all the images around me. I wish I wouldn't have tried to look at the women around me (real or otherwise) from a man's perspective, and viewed them as competition.

If I would have focused more on God's love and care for me instead of trying to be what I thought Tim wanted, things would have been so much easier my children and me. I can see now how sad it was for my girls to watch Tim and me fight, watch me cry (a lot), and watch Tim go away. My girls watched me change from looking motherly to wearing tight jeans and working out all the time. We would have all been so much better off had understood how to draw near to God. But this is something for which I have forgiven myself, and I have asked forgiveness from God and my older children. If you are there, it is okay. We all handle things the best we possibly can with the information we have at the time. I am suggesting, though, that it will be helpful to you if you learn from my mistakes.

Counselor's Corner

You, like Tina, might be beating yourself for doing things wrong. Most churches, pastors, and even family counselors don't often have the most helpful approach when it comes to sexual addiction. So put the whip down and give yourself grace. What I love about Tina is her heart to learn and incorporate new understanding into her healing journey. Regardless of where you are, God can always help you adjust and readjust.

Tina, like most wives, ends up taking her husband on as project. That is the last thing he needs! The conclusion he will come to: "Shame on me; something is wrong with me and she wants to fix me." Remember, the shame of feeling there has been something wrong with him drives the addiction. Guilt says I have done something wrong. Shame says there is something wrong with me; I am flawed. The enemy lies to him and heaps on the shame. I love Jesus' response to shame:

*...let us lay aside every weight, and the sin which so easily ensnares us, and let us run with endurance the race that is set before us, looking unto Jesus, the author and finisher of our faith who for the joy that was set before Him endured the cross, **despising the shame,** and has sat down at the right hand of the throne of God.*
Hebrews 12: 1b-2 (NKJ)-emphasis added

Some translations say Jesus refused the shame. We are all to run the race refusing the shame. The best way to do that is to have good God-esteem. We all, wife and the addict, need to reprogram our beliefs about ourselves; the enemy from day one has tried to make us believe there is something wrong with us.

Because our limbic (survival) brain was programed by age six through experiences, the only way to change the negative things we believe about ourselves is through new God-experiences. Tina kept trying to be what she thought Tim wanted and began to lose sight of who God created Tina to be.

My challenge to you is: Who has God created you to be? I was able to discover who God created me to be when I began to look at the things I struggled with. The enemy knows our gifting and that is where he will attack. I struggled with a negative, critical spirit. As I tried hard to change and not be critical and negative, God spoke to my heart and said, " Diane, I don't give you power to *not* be something; I give you power to become who I have called you to be." He took me to Galatians 5:22. As I looked at the fruit of the Spirit the word "kindness" jumped out at me. I heard God say, "Diane, I have called you to be a gracious woman of God." To be honest, I laughed. I had never seen that modeled in my family of origin. How was I to walk in something I had never experienced? I sensed the Lord saying that if I yield this area to Him and ask the Holy Spirit to be my guide and help, He will mentor and teach me to walk in the Spirit rather than the flesh. Sure enough, every time I was about to be negative or critical I would sense the Holy Spirit whispering, "Diane, let's go this way instead."

Who has God called you to be, especially in this season where the enemy will try to get you to be a cheap copy of someone else? Or the enemy will try to have you react to your husband's addiction in ways that don't represent your Christian values. I am not saying there won't be times when you will need to express your anger and hurt. The need to find your voice and express your feelings is good. The key is the attitude in which you express those feelings.

I encourage you to look at the fruit of the Spirit. If you struggle with any of the attitudes or behaviors listed in the right column, God may be revealing to you that He has called you to be just the opposite.

Galatians 5:22: The Fruit of the Spirit

Fruit	Unwanted Attitudes & Behaviors
Love	unforgiveness, anger, bitterness, judgmental
Joy	depression, heaviness, loneliness, hopelessness
Peace	anxiety, fear, control
Patience	easily irritated, frustration, perfectionism, over react
Kindness/Goodness	Negative, critical, judgmental
Faithfulness	riddled by fear, continually controlling rather than trusting God
Self-Control	compulsive or impulsive, out-of-control areas

❤ *Who has God called you to be, especially in this season of betrayal? Write out your thoughts in your journal.* Then *speak a prayer of surrender over that area to the Holy Spirit. Ask Him to help you walk in the fruit that is opposite of your struggle.*

Remember: When betrayal happens, it is normal for you to feel anger and find it hard to forgive. Working through anger and forgiveness is a process, and it will take time. In fact, in our *Betrayal & Beyond* workbooks we don't even deal with anger and forgiveness until we are six months into the healing process. But asking the Holy Spirit to soften your heart and help you begin the process of forgiveness is important. In the next chapter Tina shares how her anger surfaced, how she began to find her voice, and her decision to use her anger towards positive ends—to help other women struggling with sexual betrayal. Also, chapter 8 in this book will give you more helps in working through this process.

Many women I have worked with find themselves identifying with Peace and Faithfulness. Despite their fear of the future and their husband's behavior, they realize God has called them to walk as a woman of Faith in His Peace rather than being controlled by fear. Learning to walk by Faith and Peace is so difficult they realize they can only be victorious through the power of the Holy Spirit.

❤ *Journal which of the fruit of the Spirit you believe God is calling you to and why.*

Part of walking in a new way is learning to guard your heart as Proverbs 4:23 (NLT) says: *Guard your heart above all else, for it determines the course of your life.*

❤ *From what are guarding your heart? Journal using some of the Scripture below.*

Proverbs

5:12	A heart that despises correction
6:18	A heart that devises wicked plans
7:9-10	A heart of cunning
12:20	A heart of deception
14:10	A heart of bitterness
18:12	A heart of pride
19:3	A heart that rages against the Lord

❤ *What type of heart do you desire to cultivate? Journal responses to some of the following scriptures:*

1 Kings 3:9	An understanding heart
Psalm 51:10	A clean heart
Psalm 51:17	A broken and contrite heart
Psalm 119:11	A heart that treasures God's Word
Proverbs 17:9	A joyful heart
John 14:1	An untroubled heart

Chapter 7

Finding My Voice: Boundaries and Expectations

We now have this light shining in our hearts, but we ourselves are like fragile clay jars containing this great treasure. This makes it clear that our great power is from God, not from ourselves. We are pressed on every side by troubles, but we are not crushed. We are perplexed, but not driven to despair. We are hunted down, but never abandoned by God. We get knocked down, but we are not destroyed.
2 Corinthians 4:7-9 (NLT)

Thoughts from my journals:

I can't seem to find my peace. I feel so angry towards Tim all the time.

My life is not bad. It is good. My kids are healthy. Thank God. We have a roof over our heads and enough to eat. But I am so lonely I could just die.

Sometimes I really do want to just disappear. I think everyone would be so much better off if I was out of the picture. Then Tim could live with his fantasies. I am so sick of letting everyone down and being such a bad example.

I took Doug's advice and went to the Every Heart Restored workshop, choosing the first one I could find. I was relieved that it was a plane ride away as I needed that time on the plane to think. When I arrived at the hotel a bit early, I sat in the lobby and watched people. I wondered how many of the women walking in were there to register for the workshop; I wondered how many of the men staying at the hotel without their wives were planning to be unfaithful to them this weekend. I was angry, afraid, and excited. When the New Life registration table was set up, I was one of the first to sign up. I immediately felt safe as the friendly staff welcomed me. After registering I resumed watching people. I wondered if the many women who looked sad were here for the same reason I was. I ached for them, wanted to hug them, and tell them that we would be okay.

Before long a beautiful woman with New Life materials in her hand sat near me. After introducing myself and talking for a few minutes, I asked her about herself and she told me that her husband had been to the Every Man's Battle workshop and now they were going to the Couples Recovery part of the workshop. She shared that they were missionaries from Alaska and that their church was funding the weekend for them. I was shocked on so many levels. First, she was gorgeous; second, they were missionaries; and third…they were missionaries! How could this affect a missionary? They were people of God!

Later that day we met with the staff for a meet and greet. Since everyone seemed wonderful, I was sure that I was in the right place. When it was time for the first session, I made sure to sit at the front. I didn't want to miss anything! I wanted to be able to leave this weekend completely healed and happy. I only had three days to get well and I didn't want ANY distractions. Stephen Arterburn spoke on his book *"Healing is a Choice."* He was funny and wonderful, but he was a man and I hated him. I hated him because, in my mind, he represented **every other man** who was out to take advantage of women. Stephen's beautiful young wife was at the workshop with him, accompanied by their new son. When I saw how young and beautiful she was I just *knew* that he had traded his "old" wife for this new, younger one. (Not true at all. They have an incredible story). Just like all men, I rationalized, he wanted something better, and because he was a man, he would get what he wanted.

After the first session we were directed to meet with our group and our counselor. All the women in my group were smart and beautiful, and several of them were married to ministers. Even though they were elegant, poised, and successful, every one of them was in a place of tremendous pain. I heard stories that made me angry, stories that made me cry, and stories that I could relate to so well.

Throughout the weekend the main sessions were helpful, but I learned the most from these brave women. I learned that the pain is so real. I learned it is natural to hurt, acceptable to scream, and wonderful to cry with friends. I learned that my husband was not a pervert, I had no reason to be embarrassed, and that I was not alone. I WAS NOT ALONE! I-WAS-NOT-ALONE! Sometimes the amount of anger in the room was overwhelming, but the compassion that came next was incredibly healing. We were all at different places in our lives and we all had our own perspectives, but in the end, we were all bound by the fact that every one of us had been betrayed by the man that we loved the most, the man who promised protection, love, and honor. He was the father to our children, the one we sat by at church, the one who was supposed to keep us safe. He was not supposed to be the one who brought so much incredible pain. We were all scared and angry, and we were all there for answers. Every one of us wanted to know the same thing, "What next?"

I would love to tell you that I left that weekend healed, and ready to face life with a smile—but I would be lying. I boarded that plane to go back to my family even more confused and angry and with just as much apprehension as I had when I left home for the workshop. The difference now was that I knew that I was not alone. I knew that it truly was not about me, even though every fiber in my being screamed that it was. (This fact has taken me years to truly grasp. And even now I struggle with it at times). I left the New Life weekend ready to fight for all the wonderful women I had met. I determined I was going to heal from all this because one day I wanted to be a voice. One day I would stand up and scream for all the women just beginning this battle who thought they were all alone. I would shout that they were not alone! It was not about them! They *could* survive this! The New Life weekend gave me my voice and a purpose and a goal to work toward.

Thoughts from my journal:

Tim asked me this morning if I would ever be happy again. I can't imagine ever being happy again.

He said he is holding me back from happiness, that maybe I should leave. Maybe I should. I will never be sexy to him. I will never be enough. I am so lonely. Truth is, I just want the pain to stop.

Truth is, right now I hate him so much.

When I got home from the weekend Tim seemed a bit scared. I was happy to see my children again, but I didn't really want to see Tim. I think he was expecting me to come back ready to move on and walk beside him, but I wasn't. I was angry and resentful and I wanted nothing to do with him. My plan was to work on me and let him work on him; I would spend more time with my kids and not worry about what he did or didn't do. Tim seemed angry about my new attitude and more than once he commented that I was "supposed to come back happy." At this point I didn't care if our marriage made it or not; I thought I would be fine without him. The Bible did say that I could leave him if he was unfaithful, right? But even though I was angry, and even though I felt that my anger was justified, I still loved Tim. I still wanted him to look at me and tell me that I was the only one for him and that he would never look at another. I still wanted him to rescue me from this pain and tell me it would be ok.

I continued to look for proof that Tim was not acting out. Somewhere I heard that a man needs sex every three days, so when that third day came and still no sex, I was sure that Tim had acted out. I started keeping track on the calendar of the days that we fooled around and then I would look for "proof" that he was not being faithful. One night when I saw Tim at the computer and he was touching the top of the screen, I started crying, my knees became weak, and I felt like I couldn't move. Seeing him touch the computer screen like that made me think I had walked in on him caressing his lover. I made it to the bathroom and cried like I have never cried before. Tim came in, looked at me, then turned around and walked out. At that moment all I wanted him to do was hold me, tell me he loved me, and promise me that he would never betray me again, but at that moment he couldn't. He was wondering why I didn't trust him yet since it had been three months. He indicated I should trust him, but I didn't. I couldn't because to forgive him meant to forget and to forget meant that I could be taken off guard and hurt again. I knew I could not survive going through this again. And trust? Would I ever trust him again?

Tim continued to read his Bible every morning, and then he would read to me from a devotional book and pray out loud with me. At first I was resentful as he read and prayed, thinking he was pretending to be something that I knew he wasn't; but over time I started paying attention to his prayers. He prayed for our marriage and for God to help him guard his eyes. His prayers became sincere pleas to God to make him be a godly man, a better dad, and worthy of my love. I found myself looking forward to his prayers because in them I heard his heart. In his prayers I learned the many ways that God was working in his life, and I found myself wanting what he had—a sincere desire to please God and be what He created me to be. So I began reading and praying more. My heart was softening toward Tim and I found myself wanting to be around him.

Thoughts from my journal:

This morning Tim took my face in his hands, looked me straight in the eyes—with tears in his eyes—and said, "I—love—you—Tina." He loves me. He really loves me!

It takes time, but eventually something will happen, something will be said, that gives hope, that lets us see a glimpse of God working in our lives. We will feel a light in us as we open up to God and allow Him to work in our hearts. Over time the pain will start to lessen and you, too, will be able to start to not hate your husband so much. And you will start to feel some joy again.

On the airplane ride back from the New Life weekend, I journaled a letter to Tim that helped me begin to express my anger, find my voice, express truths about myself and my value:

Tim,

I am angry with you because it seemed to me that you never thought about my needs/wants. I cried out to you so many times and you ignored me. I feel betrayed. You had multiple affairs and expect to get off with an "I'm sorry." From my perspective, our entire marriage has been "all about Tim." Tim isn't happy so we move. Tim isn't happy so we all walk around on eggshells trying to make him happy. Tim gets disappointed so he ignores the kids as they beg continuously for his forgiveness. If Tim doesn't want to do something or talk about something, we don't.

You don't communicate respect for me. If I want to do something outside of our family (Bible study, teach Sunday school) you don't deem worthy, you point out that I don't have time and need to watch my priorities. But you don't think twice about volunteering me to dog sit or babysit, or to do/make things for people you know. If you respected me, you would take better care of yourself; I am tired of watching you slowly kill yourself by stress and no exercise. You can be a bully, shoving your weight around and swinging or punching at the kids, staying just far enough away to not hit them. You lie to the kids and me continuously, even if you consider it simply an exaggeration.

I pray that your transformation is real and lasting. And I pray you stay humble. I pray you learn to love and to forgive. I pray that you keep trying and praying and reading and growing.

I have a right to expect a husband who loves me, respects me, and honors our marriage. I have a right to ask for sex and get it, even if you are "not in the mood." I don't like sex from behind…. From behind I feel like the hole for your porn, and that you can imagine anyone you want to be with because you can't see my face. I want someone—you—to make love to ME. I no longer want to feel cheap.

Your typical behavior right now would be to pout and get angry, anything to put this on me and punish me for making you feel bad. But I don't care. I am tired of feeling guilty for my anger. I am tired of kissing up to you, and I am tired of it being "all about Tim." If you feel bad, you deserve to feel bad. YOU betrayed me. YOU lied to me. YOU allowed me to believe there was something wrong with ME. You even encouraged me to feel that way by not speaking up when counselors put our problems on me. Did you EVER look into my eyes? That last counselor almost had me suicidal! YOU left me lying alone in bed—waiting—while YOU jacked off to some whore on the computer!

I pray that you don't return to your addiction out of anger. I pray that your covenant of purity is with God and not just some group of men. I pray that you never lie to me again—

ever. And I pray that if you do return to your junk that God will give me the discernment to know, even before you tell me, even if you never do.

One thing I learned this weekend is that I am a very strong woman. I am a bright, beautiful, amazing woman and I CAN make it on my own. There is absolutely no doubt that I would do well ON MY OWN. And I refuse to be second best. I will not allow Satan back in our home through porn. And I will remove whatever is allowing him in, be it the computer, the TV, and/or you.

I NEED it in writing that you understand what you have done. I NEED it in writing that you know that you are a sex addict, and that you understand the character traits that go along with being an addict (manipulation, lying, controlling, secretive, bullying). And I need it in writing that you realize that if this ever returns to my home it will be removed, and I will ask you to leave. I need it in writing that you will continue your group, talk with a counselor regularly, and find out where this comes from before it takes another form, and that you will do weekly accountability and that you will continue to read and study how to MAKE THIS RIGHT.

You have come a long way and I am proud of you. I am one of the few women whose husband is repentant. But I have been hurt; YOU have hurt me, probably more then you could EVER know, and in order for me to trust you again I NEED these things from you. If you are not willing, or try to make me feel bad for requesting them, then I will know you are not truly repentant. If you are not truly repentant, it will happen again, and I will NOT be hurt again. Nor will I allow my daughters to be treated the way daughters of porn addicts are treated.

We all have choices. I have made mine; now it's your turn.

Tina

At the Every Heart Restored workshop I met some women who found out about their husbands addictions years ago.

These poor women had gone through years of their husbands' promising to be faithful and then acting out again. Some of their husbands were deeply sorry when their wives found out, yet some of them really didn't see why it was such a big deal. I was so angry to hear their stories of repeated betrayal as these poor wives waited on pins and needles for the next confession to come. They were tired and overwhelmed and they didn't know what to do. They were wonderful women, strong and courageous, and they extended such grace to their husbands, grace I was not willing to extend to mine. What was my advice to those women at the time? "Get out! Leave him! You deserve so much better!!!" I was angry for them, and resolved I would not live my life wondering when the news would come that would start this hurtful process all over again. If Tim acted out again, I would leave him. I didn't need him; the kids and I would be fine on our own. Now, I am not advocating this kind of attitude, but I do want to share something with you by James Dobson, from his book *Love Must Be Tough:*

> Only those who have been rejected by a beloved spouse can fully comprehend the tidal wave of pain that crashes into one's life when a relationship ends. Nothing else matters. There are no consoling thoughts. The future is without interest or hope. Emotions swing wildly from despair to acceptance and back again. Nothing in human experience can compare with the agony of knowing that the person to whom you pledged eternal devotion has betrayed your trust and is now involved in sexual intimacies with a "stranger"…a competitor…a more beautiful or handsome playmate. Death itself would be easier to tolerate than being tossed aside like an old shoe.[19]

Dobson goes on to say that when the rejected partner panics and tries to hold on to the one who cheated by begging, pleading, and crying, the cheater loses respect for the rejected spouse. He advocates following the Apostle Paul's advice in 1 Corinthians 7:15, "But if the unbeliever leaves, let him do so. A believing man or woman is not bound in such circumstances; God has called us to live in peace." Dobson points out that we could no more have gotten our spouses to ask us to marry them by begging and pleading than we can get them to stay. He suggests pointing out to your spouse that you still love him and wish to work on your marriage, but if he does not wish to get help or work on your marriage, he is free to go. Ok, so it sounds like game playing to me, but looking back, that is exactly what I did. Is that why my marriage is still intact? I don't know. But I do know that the confidence that I gained in telling Tim that I would not tolerate him returning to his addiction was immeasurable. And, in turn, I think I did earn his respect.

No program, whether it is Every Man's Battle or Pure Desire, can guarantee your marriage will stay intact. Both programs agree it will take hard work on the addict's part. He has for years been caught up in this addiction and he will have to choose to renew his brain and walk in restoration. If he chooses not to work on getting healthy and if he is being abusive—physically, emotionally, or sexually—it is important for you to come up with a safety plan. (Some helps for a safety plan are included in the resource section of this book.) Counseling under these circumstances is a must. With the help of a Christian counselor and/or pastor, separation may be an appropriate course to take, especially if you are facing danger or abuse. If separation takes place, the ideal would be for both you and your spouse to receive help. If he chooses not to get counseling, it is paramount that you get counseling so you can make good decisions about boundaries and your future.

I made many mistakes because I didn't know what to do, but looking back I can see a number of positive and important decisions I did make:

- I searched for resources on sexual addiction and began educating myself.
- I sought a counselor (Doug, whom I have mentioned) to use as a sounding board for my reactions, boundaries, and choices.
- I went to a group that helped me understand I was not alone and that I didn't have to try and become someone I wasn't.
- I found my voice and confronted Tim with what it was going to take for me to regain trust and make our marriage work.

Through educating myself, I learned that trust is earned. Tim couldn't understand why I didn't trust him after three months. I learned it takes up to two years to restore trust when a spouse has been unfaithful. The following information will give you some ideas about how trust can be restored.

First, your husband has to be completely honest. He must confess the whole truth. He must make sure that there is nothing left untold that, if found out, would make him seem untrustworthy. And he must not make excuses for his addiction. He must take full responsibility for his actions and not blame you or others. Some women need a polygraph every three to six months to establish a baseline of truth. (See information in the resource section at the back of this book for more information about the polygraph.)

Second, he must be completely open. He should allow you complete access to his life—cell phone, computer, mail, everything. Covenant Eyes on all electronics (computers, smart phones, etc.) allows other men, mentors and or a Pure Desire leader to know everywhere he has gone on the internet. And he must answer all your questions openly and honestly about where he has been, who he has been with, etc. Complete openness. No secrets allowed! This part is very difficult for men, but is crucial in rebuilding trust.

He must be compassionate and patient with you. He needs to realize that he has hurt you greatly and it is going to take time to heal and trust again. And if he does slip, real remorse and sorrow must be real. He must also be willing to abide by natural consequences that you have stated before hand if he relapses. He must demonstrate complete openness and repentance.

Your husband will probably hate this part of his recovery. Rebuilding trust takes a lot of work. But you can't do your part until he does his. He must be consistent and faithful in his actions. If he says that your lack of trust is your problem, then he does not understand the healing process and how deeply he has hurt you.

Even if your husband is in a group, it may take a few months for him to understand the depth of wounding you have gone through and the depth of repentance he needs to acknowledge to you. The Bible tells us that in-depth healing will come when people confess fully: *"Therefore confess your sins to each other and pray for each other so that you may be healed. The prayer of a righteous person is powerful and effective"* (James 5:16).

I am saddened now to see how alone and confused I was several years ago. I wanted to curl up into a little ball and die. (Or at least hide until the pain went away.) I have struggled not to feel guilty for the things I did and the people I neglected during that time. I have learned through the years that I need to ask forgiveness and then forgive myself for the things I did because of my hurt. I have learned, and am still learning, that I cannot just "work" my way through healing and I cannot do it alone. I grew up thinking that if I just tried harder or was a better person then things would turn out fine. I thought that as long as I had control kept it all inside I could handle things on my own. But I now know that being transparent and open with God as well as others allows me to receive strength and healing. I find joy and beauty in watching women in the

Betrayal & Beyond Group I lead share their struggles with each other and support one another. They are free to express their hurts, anger, and confusion and through this process they find strength and healing. These women pray for each other and help one another to see they are not alone and there is nothing wrong with them.

A darling and beautiful young woman in my group told me the thing that hurts her the most is her husband choosing other women over her. She was able to share her fears in our group of women who could completely understand her story. No one judged her. Everyone could relate and share in her pain, as well as offer encouragement and remind her of the truth: it is not about her and it is not that he wants the other women more than her.

I used to think that if I kept my feelings and fears away from my children then they would be better off. I tried to separate myself into two people: the mom who smiled and made everything fine and the grieving wife who went into a back room and cried. But I now know that this does not work. I was so full of grief and suffering that I spent more time isolated then with my children.

When I recently got the call that my father had died in a military convalescent hospital, my family and I were at Six Flags celebrating the New Year. I pretended that everything was fine, told the kids of his death matter-of-factly (they never knew him), and then went about the day. Every once in a while I would see them look over at me with concerned looks on their faces, but after a smile from me they would return to the fun of the day. When we got back to the car and started on our way home, I felt free to begin grieving since the kids could not see me from their seats in the back of the car. I cried silently, hoping that no one would notice. Through my pain, I heard my phone alert me I had received a text from my nineteen-year-old daughter. "Mommy, I love you. Is there anything that I can do?" it read. A few minutes later I felt hands reach through the back of my seat, gently rubbing my shoulders. They were the loving hands of my fifteen-year-old daughter telling me that she was there for me. Two more encouraging and loving texts from my grown daughters who had heard about the death from their siblings came through my phone as I realized I was not alone.

By the time I got home I felt free to "not be ok." I walked over to my husband, put my head on his chest and started to cry. And guess what? He held me. He held me and just let me cry. He was there for me and it felt wonderful. I was able to let my guard down and say, "I need you." Later that day, I was in the kitchen and my ten-year-old daughter walked into the room, looked at me and said, "Mommy are you ok?" I told her I was sad but that I would be fine and that I really needed a hug right now. She walked over to me, held me in her little arms, and let me cry. After a couple of minutes, she patted me on the head and smiled at me. She had helped and she felt good about it. Let them be there for you; don't stop being present. It is ok not to be ok as long as you are not depending on them for your healing.

Counselor's Corner

Tina's letter to Tim is powerful for a number of reasons. First, she pointed out her value and how she needed him to value her in return; she needed to be loved, respected, and honored, not only as a wife, but also as a human being. Second, she shared how hurtful his actions were both emotionally and sexually. Part of processing your pain and being honest with your spouse is sharing the hurtful things that have happened in your sexual times together. The third important component to Tina's letter is her telling what she needed from him and what the natural consequences would be if he continued to relapse. She essentially created a safety plan (Look in the resource section of this book for an example of a safety plan adapted from *Betrayal & Beyond Book 2*.)

Just as you are involved in learning to forgive through this process, your husband needs to learn how to repent. Most men do not understand the depth of wounding, how long it will take to trust, and how they must continue to validate your feelings as you are going through this process. An excellent resource to help you to articulate your needs is found in a book by Linda J. MacDonald, *How to Help Your Spouse Heal From Your Affair*. I recommend this for our clients even if the addiction is porn and masturbation. The information in this book helps the husband understand that he can rebuild the marriage and relationship, but it will require a lot of work. Linda presents the Three R's:

Resilience: He will have to withstand all of the wife's emotional ups and downs—her emotions will be like a roller coaster.

Realistic: It will take time to rebuild trust and experience her full forgiveness.

Respectful: The husband should respect the wife's choices on how to proceed through the healing process and be willing to do whatever it will take for healing to come.[20]

❤ *Journal some thoughts about what you would need to see your husband doing in order for him to begin to gain your trust.*

• **Disclosure is another aspect Tina touches upon**. What do you share with your children? *Disclosing Secrets*[21] is an excellent resource that we cite in *Betrayal & Beyond Book 1*.[22] The information needs to come from you and not someone else.

- Some helpful guidelines from the Betrayal & Beyond summary of disclosure with children include:

- Age appropriateness. I suggest to our counseling clients that children age eight and under understand lying. Saying; "Daddy has been lying to mommy and that has made her sad," is very appropriate for this age group.

- Be guided by the child's desire to know. Let them determine the level of disclosure.

- Assure the children you are getting help in this recovery process so they don't instinctively try to care-take.

- Provide emotional support for the children after the disclosure through the church or a therapist.

- Teach about healthy sexuality out of what you are learning. The Pure Desire website has a resource for parents listing age appropriate books for teaching about healthy sexuality from a Christian perspective.

- If your child is struggling in life, wait for disclosure until you, as a couple, are in agreement that the time is right.

Chapter 8

Battle Scars and Forgiveness

Thoughts from my journal:

I am so sick of not trusting Tim and questioning everything!

It's amazing the fluctuation of emotions that I feel.

As I look back over the years of rejection, were they anything compared to what is happening to Tim now?

I can honestly say I am happy again. I enjoy my children and I love my husband with a deepness that I never knew existed. But it has been a long road. Things would be going fine and then I would see a pretty girl walk by him and instantly I would hate Tim. I would get angry if we happened to walk by a Victoria's Secret store together, even though he would make it a point to walk with his back to the building, never even glancing in the store's direction. Or if we were at a bookstore and I happened to see a swimsuit magazine nearby, I would begin to wonder if he had seen it, assume he had, then I would become angry and hateful. To be honest, he wouldn't even have to be at the store with me for me to get angry at him. I would simply assume he had seen the magazine at another store. But Tim doesn't look anymore. He makes it a point to look away and "take every thought captive" (2 Corinthians 10:5). He plays with our girls and puts our family ahead of everything, always making us feel like we are the most important people in the world to him. Tim works hard to maintain a balance in his life. I am very proud of the husband and father he has become.

Tim was willing to do *anything* toward healing. This

angered me terribly in the beginning, but I really think it was probably the best attitude he could have taken. He would leave the room if someone walked in who was dressed immodestly, turn his head during movie scenes that he thought might compromise his thoughts, and would not rent any movie that had the words "sex" or "sensuality" in the rating or description. He had safeguards installed on the computer for which only I had the password, and he made sure that someone was in the room if he did go on the computer at home. One time we were out shopping and Tim saw from quite far away that the checkout girl was not dressed appropriately, so he called for me from across the store so that I could check out for him. At first I was annoyed, but as I thought about how truly thoughtful Tim was being, I became quite proud of him. He once told me of a business meeting he attended where he actually kept his back turned to a female colleague because she was dressed questionably. At first I thought this was rude, but then I thought about the woman. Wasn't she being rude by dressing in a way that would cause husbands to stumble?

Tim avoided going on travel for work because he knew the hotels would be a problem. Sometimes it is unavoidable, so he devised a plan. First he wrote me a contract. Yes, a contract that I wish to share with you.

I, Timothy Harris, being of sound mind, promise to adhere to the following criteria while on travel:

1. *Contact my beautiful wife daily and convey my thoughts and share any concerns that I might have, particularly with my recovery.*

2. *Ensure that my wife is the last person that I speak with each day while away.*

3. *Have the hotel manager contact my wife and confirm the TV removal during the course of my stay.*

4. *I promise to adhere to my daily battle plan with extra*

diligence, i.e. reading, bouncing of the eyes, exercise, etc.

5. *Speak daily with one of my fellow soldiers in recovery.*

6. *If any strange or abnormal feelings or thoughts come to mind, I will call my wonderful wife and share them.*

7. *I also will ensure that my travel is as short as possible.*

These items I promise to perform.

Signed: Timothy Harris, Your husband

A bit extreme? Maybe. But do you think I was worried while he was away? Well, yes, of course I was, but not as much as I would have been had he not taken the initiative to create the contract. Tim has taken Job 31:1 seriously: *"I made a covenant with my eyes not to look lustfully at a woman."*

Thoughts from my journal:

I analyze Tim's every action. I try to make everyone happy. Meanwhile I want to run away.

I am so tired. I'm not sure what I am so tired of. I just want to go to bed and not wake up for a very long time.

If we were not together, I would spend more time and energy with my girls, I would start dressing more modestly because there wouldn't be anyone to try to impress, and I would be a better example.

Counselors and recovery specialists say healing takes at least two years. When I heard this I was completely overwhelmed. I did not think I could survive two years of this. But it's not two years of solid pain, it is a process of two steps forward, one step back. I would think that everything was fine and then I would talk to someone or see something and I would feel that I was right back at the beginning. In the beginning it took a while to recover from these setbacks, but over time it became easier. Over time I became less affected by what I heard or saw. It was difficult to not blame Tim for every sexy woman who walked by, for me not to think he was like a kid in a candy store every time a group of scantily clad young girls walked by. Here he would be "bouncing his eyes" and I would be angry at him that these girls even passed by.

I specifically remember one time when we went out as a family to a Renaissance Festival. We were all so excited to go and paid a good price for admission. We walked around for a while learning about the time period, our girls enjoying the wonderful sights and smells. Since almost every woman we passed had her chest almost completely exposed, Tim looked at the ground and me, ready to lose it! I excused myself to the bathroom, called my sister on my cell phone, and started to cry, "I feel like I've stepped into hell! And Tim is walking around in heaven!"

Over the next few hours I became angrier and angrier, blaming Tim every time a woman walked by in next to nothing. I became so angry that I could no longer walk beside him. I started to think that he brought us here on purpose. *He knew what would be here,* I told myself. *He just wanted an acceptable way to look at porn, and he brought our whole family into it.* Our girls, however, thought it was all quite amusing. Before long Tim excused himself to the car as I finished up the festival with our girls. I cried inside as I thought about what he may have been doing with the images he had seen, the visual "snapshots" he may have taken. When I got to the car, I could not even look at Tim, I hated him so badly. During the long car ride home he told me how hard it had been to bounce his eyes, as there was nowhere he could bounce them to. He told me he wrestled with the idea of telling us that we needed to leave the moment we walked through the gates, but he didn't want to let the girls down or make me angry we had wasted so much money. He assured me that no visual snapshots were taken, and apologized for taking us there in the first place. By the time we got home my anger had almost subsided and I was able to be amused at the horrible display we had seen. I learned that day that my perception was not the same as Tim's, and I vowed to try to extend a bit more grace.

The road ahead is a long one, and it will not be easy. But as I have reviewed all of my old journals and remembered the pain, I realize how much God has blessed me. At the time I did not think I could survive; I would be lying if I told you I did not have battle scars. But the closeness I now share with my husband and my God far outweigh the pain I went through during those first two years. I would never want to go through them again, but if had to do that again, I would know that God can and will carry me through them, if I let Him. I would know that someday God would turn my sorrow into dancing (Psalm 30:11). I would know that somewhere there would be women just like me who would need to learn from my pain and would draw from the strength they saw God give me, when they were in too much pain to see Him for themselves.

I wish more than anything that I could take away your pain. I wish I could reach over and give you a hug and tell you that everything would be okay, that your story would end up like mine. But I can't. I can tell you that I was where you are and there are many women right there with you. YOU ARE NOT ALONE! I can tell you my story and tell you that God is with you. HE WILL NOT LEAVE YOU! And years later when you look back on this time, you will see the times that He carried you when you were too weak or overwhelmed to continue.

There *is* hope, but this battle is ongoing. Sometimes a comment or situation triggers more anger than is appropriate; little things can make me question my husband's integrity and I go back into my old pain. The sad, overwhelming feeling will start to go away, then the anger. Then one day you will wake up and realize that you are living again and you will be able to say, "I SURVIVED!"

I had to hang onto Jeremiah 29:11-13 and repeat it over and over: "For I know the plans I have for you," declares the Lord, "plans to prosper you and not to harm you, plans to give you hope and a future. Then you will call upon me and come and pray to me and I will listen to you. You will seek me and find me when you seek me with all your heart."

I hated hearing about forgiveness, and I hated anyone who was smug enough to even suggest that I forgive Tim; I was certain that if they were in my shoes they would feel the same as I did. I feel like I am betraying you by even suggesting you forgive your husband. Yes, he screwed up; yes, you hurt so bad you probably struggle just to face each day; and, no, he probably doesn't deserve to be forgiven. But without forgiveness you will be trapped in your pain and anger. Without forgiveness the pain will get bigger and bigger and resentment and bitterness will seep in and build a wall between you and God. You will be the miserable one. Forgiveness will not be easy, quick, or permanent, but will be an ongoing struggle that you will need to release to God every day. You may think you have forgiven your husband, and then something will happen that brings you right back to the place of unforgiveness. This may make you question your sincerity and your walk with God. Forgiveness, like an onion, has many layers; it is only in removing one layer that you can see into the next. Be patient with yourself and the process. Right now you have two choices: to forgive and move on or forgive and stay. Not forgiving cannot be an option, as it will end up killing you and damaging your family and Satan could outwit us: "I have forgiven in the sight of Christ…in order that Satan might not outwit us, for we are not unaware of his schemes (2 Corinthians 2:10)."

Forgiveness does not mean forgetting, nor does it mean pretending that nothing happened. If I forgave Tim, I reasoned, he would be released to hurt me again. Biblical forgiveness requires that you first admit that you were hurt. It means telling your husband how badly he hurt you, admitting to yourself how you feel, and allowing yourself to feel the pain.

"When we forgive someone, we do not forget the hurtful act, as if forgetting came along with the forgiveness package the way strings come with a violin. Begin with the basics. If you forget, you will not forgive at all. You can never forgive people for things you have forgotten about. You need to forgive precisely because you have not forgotten what someone did; your memory keeps the pain alive long after the actual hurt has stopped. Remembering is your storage of pain. It is why you need to be healed in the first place," wrote Lewis Smedes.[23] Remembering helps you to notice the red flags later; it is *not* remembering that is harmful. Bitterness and resentment build up when we don't release our husbands to God and choose instead to punish them and make them pay for their mistakes. "Make sure that nobody pays back wrong for wrong, but always try to be kind to each other and to everyone else" (1 Thessalonians 5: 15).

My pain was like a jacket of resentment that I wore; I would take it off for a bit, but as soon as I would start to feel comfortable with Tim again, I would put it back on. Somehow I foolishly believed that as long as I was covered in my pain, I would be protected from more pain. When you live like this it keeps you from growing and healing. I like the hope that comes from Jesus' words, "Come to me, all you who are weary and burdened, and I will give you rest. Take my yoke upon you and learn from me, for I am gentle and humble in heart, and you will find rest for your souls. For my yoke is easy and my burden is light" (Matthew 11:28).

God does not ask you to forgive on your own. He will help you, if you ask.

"For if you forgive others when they sin against you, your heavenly father will also forgive you. But if you do not forgive men their sins, your Father will not forgive your sins"

(Matthew 6:14).

"Then Peter came to him and asked, "Lord, how often should I forgive someone who sins against me? Seven times?"

"No, not seven times," Jesus replied, "but seventy times seven!" (Matthew 18:21 NLT).

In the beginning I tried to tell myself that Tim's acts were no big deal; I would try to justify his offensives, thinking that it would help me forgive him if I could mentally make it all disappear. But that didn't work. Ignoring the pain or trying to "make it go away" leads to false forgiveness; if there is no pain and nothing happened, then there is nothing to forgive. Biblical forgiveness is admitting something happened, acknowledging how badly it hurt, and choosing to forgive anyway.

Tim was wonderful in asking forgiveness. He admitted what he did, apologized, and said that it would never happen again. Then he did everything within his power to ensure that it didn't. I was lucky; it is definitely easier to forgive someone who asks for your forgiveness than to forgive someone who doesn't ask. But we can forgive even if they don't ask, because forgiveness is an act of grace, a gift of love. No matter what your husband does or does not do, you are called to forgive.

I know you don't "feel" like forgiving him; you may never "feel" like it, but feelings can't think nor can they be completely trusted right now. Forgiveness is a choice, an act of will. Looking back, I see that I wasted so much time trying to "make him pay," constantly holding his offences over his head and in front of him, as though somehow it would protect me, which it did not. I grew bitter and resentful and in the end, Tim wasn't the only one punished for what he did, I punished my children as well through my unforgiveness and anger. Again, forgiveness does not mean forgetting and it does not mean trusting him again.

Childbirth can be likened to forgiveness. A point comes

near birth when you feel an overwhelming need to push. The urge is so intense there seems to be no way of stopping your body from pushing the baby out. When I was having one of my girls, the doctor said, "Tina, don't push!" To which I screamed, "I have to push!" and I meant it with every fiber of my being. But then he said, "Tina, don't push, there's a problem." Did I stop pushing? You bet I did! Was it easy? Not at all, it hurt horribly. But I chose to listen to the doctor; I mustered up every ounce of strength and determination I had in order to save my baby's life. It's the same with forgiveness. God says, "Tina, don't push!" I either choose to ignore His warning or I don't. But ultimately I end up living with the consequence of my actions. And, whether I like it or not, those actions affect many people besides just me.

Think of forgiveness like a wound. If you stepped on a piece of glass and then just tried to ignore it, there is a slight possibility that it would fall out on its own, but chances are more likely that it will stay in your foot and get embedded deeper and deeper. Every time you step, you would be in pain and eventually have to deal with infection. The pain and damage would be far greater from delaying or neglecting treatment than if you had in the beginning removed the glass, assessed the damage, cleansed the wound, and treated it with healing balm. Forgiveness is like removing the shard of glass in order to let healing take place. The wound will still hurt and the process will be difficult, but with the proper care, the wound will heal.

Counselor's Corner

Tina beautifully expressed the difficulty of walking through forgiveness. In the Betrayal &Beyond groups we wait six months to even begin that process. In *Betrayal and Beyond Book 3*, we start with grieving the loss before working through anger and forgiveness. You can't fully forgive without grieving the loss.

Joseph in the Old Testament is a great example of someone who was betrayed multiple times and went through a process of grieving and forgiving. The book of Genesis devotes nearly ten chapters to this process in Joseph's life (Genesis 40 to 50). For nearly 17 years (according to most scholars), he wrestled with the ongoing injustice of his situation without letting it control him. Then he was suddenly catapulted into a position of incredible prominence and it appeared as if God's promise to him would finally come true. But it is not fulfilled until Joseph faced the deep wounds of his past with his family. Repeatedly in the process, Joseph is emotionally troubled to the point of tears. He was a man of unlimited power and prestige who sobbed uncontrollably as he rehearsed his childhood wounds with his brothers: "He wept aloud, and the Egyptians and the house of Pharaoh heard it" (Genesis 45:2 NKJ).

Once Joseph's brothers realize the second in command in the most powerful nation in the world was the little brother who they attempted to kill, they are terrified. And Joseph allowed the hand of God to wipe his traumatic past clean when he declared, "'Don't be afraid. Do I act for God? Don't you see, you planned evil against me but God used those same plans for my good, as you see all around you right now—life for many people. Easy now, you have nothing to fear; I'll take care of you and your children.' He reassured them, speaking with them heart-to-heart" Genesis 50:19-21 (MSG).

Joseph's words full of wisdom are the doorway to your

freedom from the wounds and betrayal you have experienced. Joseph would have listed the following as issues he needed to grieve:

- Loss of safety and trust when his brothers threatened to kill him.

- Loss of his freedom when his brothers sold him into slavery.

- Loss of his family and country when he was taken to Egypt.

- Loss of his freedom again when he was put into prison because of false accusations.

Women who go through the Betrayal & Beyond workbooks share some of their losses including the following:[24]

I've lost…

_____ my joy

_____ my sense of humor

_____ the ability to trust my own inner voice

_____ my best friend

_____ my innocence

_____ the way life was

_____ dreams of ministering with my husband

_____ knowing what it would be like to be loved the way God wants me to be

_____ my family's provider

_____ my home

_____ memories; family photos bring pain now that I know

_____ a godly example for my kids

_____ self-confidence

_____ my ability to be around other women, especially pretty ones

_____ my faith in people

_____ touch, snuggles, intimate love-making

_____ financial security

_____ my future

 ***Journal your losses using ideas from this list. Like Joseph, cry out to God with regards to these losses.*** *It will help you prepare for the next chapter as Tina shares the losses that she had to process.*

Chapter Nine

Mourning & Moving On: Learning to Trust Again

Thoughts from my journals:

Lord,
My loss is nothing compared to some people's losses, and Tim says he is on the other side of this addiction, but I don't trust him. I cringe when I hear him get up in the morning, wondering what he is doing upstairs, wondering if he is acting out. I hate going out anywhere with him because of the attractive young girls he sees. (And the one in Costco—he did look at her, I saw him) I feel nauseous being around him anymore. I watch him all the time and I worry all of the time. I don't like being angry; I am even angry at my older girls because they represent what he looks at and lusts after. And I hate myself. I flirt to get attention, knowing what I am doing. Then I wonder why Tim still won't touch me. Is he masturbating again?

Lord, help me to focus on You. Help me to stop looking at Tim and his faults. Help me to look to You.

It was so hard to learn to trust Tim again. In fact, there are still days when I wonder if his gaze fell too long on a young woman, or when I find a catalogue in the mail that has bras advertised. I wonder if he looked, and then I get mad because not only do I convince myself that he did look, I also get angry at the thought that he probably enjoyed it. Tim has worked hard to regain my trust; he has made himself trustworthy by removing every temptation, by being completely transparent over the years, and by putting God and family first. I am certain that he is being completely honest and that he will probably never go back to "that place."

As you work toward trusting again, please ask God to help you see the true reality and the extent of the betrayal. Ask Him to help you to see the truth of what has happened; ask Him to reveal anything else you need to know. Scripture says, "…you may be sure that your sin will find you out" (Numbers 32:23). When you ask God to reveal the truth to you, He will; once He shows you the truth it is up to you to accept the reality of what is. As cold as this may sound, you cannot change the past; it happened and there is nothing that you can do to change that. You can scream, yell, cry, and throw things (I personally think all of these are very therapeutic), but eventually you will need to look at your situation and determine the next step, with God's help. "I can do everything through Him who gives me strength" (Philippians 4:13). Be brave enough to ask yourself some tough questions such as: Is he repentant? Has he stopped the behavior (or is he at least trying)? Is he willing to go to counseling? Is he willing to do whatever it takes to save this marriage? Am I willing to make a conscious choice to at least try to forgive and trust again?

I know that to look at the man and the betrayal can make you feel so angry the very idea of forgiveness is sickening, but we don't forgive because of our husband. We forgive because God tells us to. Period. He doesn't say that we only need to forgive some sins; He says that we need to forgive them all, again, and again, and again. So we can look at our wonderful Creator, tell Him how hard it is, and that we don't know how to do it.

When one of my daughters was a baby, I was putting her to bed one night and I looked down at her beautiful face with her wide-open eyes looking up at me. I told her it was bedtime and she needed to close her eyes and go to sleep. She squeezed them closed only to have them pop open again. Finally, she looked up at me longingly and said, "Mommy, I can't. Will you close them for me please?" Our wonderful Daddy is looking down at us and telling us we need to forgive. He understands when we say, "Lord, I can't. Will you help me please?" Like a loving parent, He will help you. "How great is the love the Father has lavished on us, that we should be called children of God!" (1 John 3:1).

We are handing them over to God when we forgive, not letting them off the hook. God will take care of them. "Do not take revenge, my friends, but leave room for God's wrath, for it is written: 'It is mine to avenge; I will repay,' says the Lord" (Romans 12:19).

You get to decide what it is that you want. If your desire is to remain married and to work on your marriage, then you can decide to do that. Satan will not like that; He does not want you and your husband together. His goal is to tear your marriage apart because he knows that "if a house is divided against itself, that house cannot stand" (Mark 3:25), so at every turn he will be throwing darts at your marriage. Remember Ephesians 6: "For our struggle is not against flesh and blood, but against the rulers, against the authorities, against the powers of this dark world and against the spiritual forces of evil in heavenly realm" (Ephesians 6:12).

Put your goal in front of you (a restored marriage) and do not look back. "But one thing I do: Forgetting what is behind and straining toward what is ahead, I press on toward the goal to win the prize for which God has called me heavenward in Christ Jesus" (Philippians 3:13). When we keep looking back we stay in the pain. But if your husband is pursuing change and you see he is being trustworthy, stop hitting him over the head with his past sin. The only way I could do this was by thinking of Tim as two different people: the past Tim (Saul on the road to Damascus) and the present Tim (my Paul, after the conversion). Just in case you aren't familiar with the story, this is a quick summary: After Jesus was crucified, had risen from the dead, hundreds of people were becoming Christ-followers. Saul was persecuting Christians, arresting and putting to death anyone who claimed to follow Jesus. While on a road to a city named Damascus, a blinding light struck him and he heard a voice telling him to stop what he was doing. For three days Saul was blind until God had a man named Ananias go to visit him. Ananias was afraid because he knew of Saul's reputation as a merciless persecutor of Christians. While Saul was praying and fasting, Ananias went to him and laid hands on him. Saul was then able to see, got up, ate, and was baptized. After his conversion Saul (who is primarily known as Paul in the New Testament) became the most determined of all the apostles of Jesus, started churches all over Asia, and ended up writing much of the New Testament (Acts 9:1-19).

Tim was a changed man, just like Saul/Paul. But like Ananias, I had to approach him with caution, because there was no way of knowing if he was going to hurt me again or if his "conversion" was a trick. Like the early Christians, I watched and prayed and waited. Tim proved trustworthy by his actions, so I began to let him into my heart little by little. By separating the two Tims, I found it easier to deal with the past. If a thought popped up—trust me, they will—I told myself that the past action was done by the past Tim, and I would try to remind myself of something trustworthy that the present Tim was doing. The Apostle Paul gives us these directions for relationships and Christian living: "We demolish arguments and every pretension that sets itself up against the knowledge of God, and we take captive every thought to make it obedient to Christ" (2 Corinthians 10:5). Just because a thought pops into your head does not mean that you need to entertain it. I wish I had understood this back in the beginning. Just because a memory would come to me did not mean that I needed to think it through until I was so sick to my stomach and I couldn't bear to look at Tim. "Finally, brothers, whatever is true, whatever is noble, whatever is right, whatever is pure, whatever is lovely, whatever is admirable—if anything is excellent and praiseworthy—think about such things" (Philippians 4:8).

You must deal with the past and mourn the loss of what you thought you had, the loss of innocence, the loss of trust, the loss of the idea that you were his one and only, the loss of the person you thought he was. You have much to mourn, so weep and seek God. Look at what Nehemiah did when he heard that the walls of Jerusalem had been broken down: "When I heard these things, I sat down and wept. For some days I mourned and fasted and prayed before the God of heaven" (Nehemiah 1:4). So mourn the loss, and then start to rebuild your life, with a new understanding.

Once everything is out in the open, you should talk openly and honestly, and listen to each other. Tell your husband what you need in order to trust him again. Make a list if you want and post it on the bedroom wall. Your list might include things like:

- I need to know where you are at every moment of every day. If you need to step out of the office please call me; if you stop at the store before coming home, let me know.
- I need you to keep a log of all the money you spend and what you buy.
- I need you to give me every password to every account that you have.
- I need to be able to look at your cell phone any time I ask.
- You must get Covenant Eyes on all your electrical devices.
- I need you to have weekly phone calls with an accountability group.
- I need you to see a counselor once a week.
- I need you to report to your accountability men things that

cause you to struggle, on a daily basis if that is what works for you. If it moves beyond temptation to sin it needs to be reported to me within 24 hours after confessing to your accountability partner.

- I need you to pray with me every day.
- I need you to have an accountability partner who will promise to tell me if you act out and you don't tell me yourself within 24 hours.
- I need you to read recovery literature every day.

There may be other things that would help you to learn to trust your husband again. Please review the Safety Plan provided in the resource section to see some suggestions. My list includes the things that I needed to help me to see that Tim was willing to change and he was making every effort.

Your husband should be open and honest with you about what he needs as well. try to not be judgmental when he tells you what he needs. Some of the things that Tim needed:

- Stop subscriptions to magazines and catalogues.
- Take down any posters of women in our daughters' rooms.
- Do not ask/require him to go to the beach or swimming pool.
- If he says he doesn't feel comfortable in a situation, remove yourselves, no questions asked. (Hopefully he will explain later.)
- Be willing to forgo any movies that he says make him uncomfortable and not rent/watch anything with a PG 13 rating or higher that lists sex or anything to do with sex in the rating.
- Be open to sex and let him see you naked. (This is only if you feel comfortable doing this. Tim said he needed this from me.)

Although it may take time and a lot of healing, one of the goals for both you and your spouse is to become intimate. The book

Sexy Christians states an important truth: Intimacy is learning to become uncomfortably close. Intimacy is not easy, especially when we have been wounded in this area. God challenges the husband to love his wife as Christ loves the church and God challenges you to respect and honor your husband (Ephesians 5: 23, 25). A man doesn't naturally know how to love his wife; he needs her to help him know her needs. The husband feels respected when the wife desires him, especially in a sexual way. Allowing Tim to look at me naked challenged me to let go of the comparisons I had been making with other women and to embrace who God made me to be. I have come to truly believe I am beautiful. Candlelight helped me become more comfortable. I have come to also believe everything looks better by candlelight!

Because of the difficult choices we both made to work towards intimacy, I love Tim so much today. I am incredibly happy and I feel valued. I can honestly say I love my life and the pain that I went through was worth experiencing to have what I now have. As your husband works to earn your trust, and you see the changes in him, your heart will start to soften toward him; you may start to notice things about him that you love and admire. You may find yourself beginning to fall in love with him all over again, only this time you will be seeing the real person, not just the one he wants you to see. When this happens, allow yourself to feel the love, see the good in him, love him again, and have fun with him. Find things that you both enjoy and go on dates again.

This process can take a long time, almost like watching a rose open. You could stare at the rose all day and not see any change. Then one day you notice the rose is fully open and more beautiful than ever. You wonder when it happened since you were right there all the time. This exchange of love letters demonstrates the opening of my rose:

Dear Tina,

I wanted to take a minute to say thank you. Yeah, I know you are asking, "For what?" As I couldn't sleep this morning, I was thinking of all the things you are to me. And I thought, Have I thanked you?

So, just a few....

- *Thank you for being at my side these years, even when it was the toughest to be.*
- *Thank you for loving me.*
- *Thank you for loving my children so much!*
- *Thank you for being by my side the closest, especially these past two years.*
- *Thank you for all your wonderful touches to our house. For example, your love for books, reading, creativity, knitting, apples, fall candy, putting the girls to bed at night and reading stories to them, and loving to learn about "computer thingies."*
- *Thank you for loving me enough to get you through the times that seemed hopeless. I can't imagine how that must have felt.*
- *Thank you for believing in our heavenly Father!*
- *Thank you for moving sooo many times.*
- *Thank you for saying "yes!"*
- *Thank you for being "drop dead" gorgeous!!*
- *Thank you for making coffee every morning!*
- *Thank you for showing me compassion.*
- *Thank you, for all that you are.*
- *Thank you for sharing your life with me!!*

God was awesome when He matched me with you. I can only hope and pray that I mean as much to you as you do to me. And I want to be able to show my gratitude for your love and dedication to our marriage.

Thank You. I love you.

Tim

Tim,

When we first met, you made me feel special. The way your eyes would light up when you saw me, the way you always seemed happy to hear my voice. The way you always seemed so proud of me in front of people you knew. Even though I had so little to offer you, you never looked down on me. You accepted me, with all my past, "as is." To me you were so brilliant, so wise, and so compassionate.

Over the years you have provided well and have tried to be what you thought was a good husband/father. I am proud of you for trying to move up at work, because that is what you thought a good husband did. I am pleased that you loved me enough to keep your struggles from me because you thought that was what you were supposed to do. I am pleased that you have supported me in raising the kids and have allowed me to home school them. But more than anything I am SO pleased and blessed that you have STOPPED trying to be what you thought was a good husband and have looked to God and have trusted Him to help you define a godly husband/father.

You have taught me TRUE faith, TRUE submission to an awesome God. You have shown me what REAL humility looks like. You have made me re-evaluate myself to God's standards, not mine, and you have made me want to be better, closer, wiser, and calmer...like you.

I commit to try to let go of the past. I commit to see you as a child of God—fully committed to God. I commit to love you with grace. FORGIVEN.

I am so blessed to have you in my life. I am so proud of your willingness and your openness. You are all I have ever wanted in a husband. I hope someday to be worthy of you.

One more thing...I think of the Song of Solomon where it says, "I am my beloveds and my beloved is mine." When I think of you now I get so excited that YOU ARE MINE! Do you remember, years ago, when I would say that it wasn't the act of sex that I wanted so badly, it was the fact that it was the

ONLY part of you that was JUST MINE? I was wrong. Now, not only have you given me the gift of having sex with only me, you also gave me something I never knew I didn't have. You gave me You. You gave me your intimacy, your heart, your trust.

Thank you.

Always yours,
Tina

Counselor's Corner

I love this beautiful exchange of love letters between Tim and Tina. These letters didn't come without pain, without working hard. These letters came because both chose to do the hard thing and that was face their greatest fear—real intimacy and vulnerability.

As Tina pointed out, being intimate is uncomfortable. Why would God in Ephesians 5 ask the husband to love the wife—which doesn't come natural—and ask the wife to respect the husband, especially sexually which for her doesn't come natural. As Ted and I share in our book *Sexy Christians*, we believe God made us this way to deal with our self-focused perspective and to learn to serve each other. God created sex as a gift, and as we begin to grow in intimacy we discover the beauty of what He had in mind.

As Tina also pointed out, establishing healthy sexuality and real intimacy takes work and time. Both the husband and wife have learned some unhealthy responses to their sexuality. We have strayed so far from what God had in mind for health in this area that many don't even know what a healthy sexual relationship between husband and wife looks like.

The following list helps us to better understand healthy sex that leads to intimacy and closeness versus unhealthy sex that destroys intimacy.[25]

Healthy Sexuality	Unhealthy Sexuality
Is respectful	Degrades & shames
Fun & exciting	Demanding & obligatory
Is victimless	Victimizes & exploits
Is intimate	Lacks emotional attachment
Mutuality in needs expressed	Needs dominated by one
Trust is foundational	Built on dishonesty
Is safe	Is unsafe, creating fear
Serves to connect emotionally	Serves to medicate pain
Creates warmth & oneness	Meets self-focused needs
Deepens values & beliefs	Compromises values & beliefs
Is authentic	Reflects a double-life

❤ *Journal about unhealthy areas in your present relationship.*

❤ *Journal two or three areas you would like to begin to work on.*

When your relationship becomes healthy enough, the chart and the above journaling questions would be important to discuss with your spouse.

| Peace Beyond the Tears

Chapter 10
Help for a Man's Hijacked Brain

Note: This chapter, including the Counselor's Corner, is written for the husband/sex addict who may be ready to begin to understand/accept some fact and truths, with the intention that the information will be read by both husband and wife.

A porn addiction recovery is very difficult. My guess is that you have tried many times to stop and every time you "act out" you vow never to do it again. You have probably cried out to God to help you stop many times, much like my husband did. Therapists say that it is more difficult to recover from a porn addiction than it is to recover from a cocaine addiction; cocaine users can get the drug out of their system, but pornographic images are in the mind and they are very easily accessible. Sexual activity outside the marriage bed literally hijacks the brain. Sexual bondage starts as a moral issue but quickly moves to a brain problem. You will read more about how that happens at the end of this chapter in the Counselor's Corner.

Shortly after Tim came home from the Every Man's Battle workshop, he disclosed everything. If you have attended the workshop, I am sure that you have been asked to do the same thing. With full disclosure, you will feel better to have everything out in the open; your wife is probably going to feel completely overwhelmed. They say that a husband's best day is his wife's worst day, and it is true. She saw her life one way, and she trusted you, and now, this man that she depended on to protect her and keep her safe, stands before her telling her that her life wasn't what she thought it was. She is likely going to doubt her entire reality and wonder what else she didn't know. You see, it is bigger than just trusting you; she is probably going to wonder why God allowed this to happen to her, and she may start to wonder how she did not know that all this was going on right under her nose. This may cause her to wonder what else she doesn't know, what is going on in other lives around her of which she is unaware. So trust will take time, patience, and much understanding.

You will rebuild her trust by being completely transparent; tell her everything that she wants to know, even if you think it is irrelevant. She is trying to build a picture that she can wrap her brain around, so don't belittle her if she asks you for the umpteenth time how old the girls were or where you met/saw them (or whatever other seemingly irrelevant question she may ask). She needs you to answer her questions openly and honestly, without making her feel stupid or crazy for asking. Yes, I know it will be hard, but think of the alternative. And try to think about how your wife is feeling. She needs you to be willing to do the difficult things for her and she needs to see that you are trustworthy. If she isn't in a group that helps her deal with her husband's sexual addiction, encourage her to get that support. She will realize she is not alone, and processing her pain with other women will help her to better know how to respond to you rather than react.

To build her trust, as well as to heal, you will need accountability. One person, definitely, but a "band of brothers" is an even better idea. My husband had both. Every Monday evening he had a phone meeting with a group of men through New Life. This phone meeting was pivotal to Tim's healing. They kept a "metrics chart" of all the things that they needed to do to "graduate" from the calls. They worked through the twelve-step program of recovery and celebrated each new victory together. They discussed their struggles and gave progress reports to each other. They committed to call each other throughout the week, especially if one of them was going on travel or having a particularly tough week. Knowing that Tim had to report to these men every Monday helped me know he was doing what he needed to do; I knew he did not want to get on the phone and tell these men he had not done what he was supposed to do from his metrics chart.

Another way to rebuild trust is to let her know you have a plan and let her see you working on it. My husband kept his metrics chart in the open where I could see it. If I had any doubt that he was doing what he needed to do, I could look at his progress. My husband's metrics chart included:

- AM/PM prayers
- Exercise
- Calls to others in the group
- Read recovery literature, such as Every Man's Battle, Every Man's Marriage, Pure Desire books or workbooks.
- Read Scripture daily

Every night he would check off that he had done these, and on his next phone meeting he would be required to tell them how many times he did each one. Before long it became a habit and after a while I stopped checking his chart to see if he had done them.

Tim had internet safety installed on our computers; if you have internet access on your phone, I strongly suggest that you install it there as well. Covenant Eyes, an accountability software, tracks every place you go on the internet; if any sites you visit have porn, this will be reported to his accountability partners, counselor, and/or group leader. Tim moved our computer out to an open area in our house and only went on it when necessary. He stopped watching any program with a rating of PG-13 or higher if sex or anything to do with sex was indicated by the rating or description. This included sports programs where the cheerleaders are wearing next to nothing.

Since Tim earnestly wanted to change and truly desired

my trust, he was willing to do just about anything to rebuild the trust in our relationship. I remember one time he went on an overnight business trip and I feared he would act out. When he got to the hotel, he had the maintenance man follow him up to the room to remove the cable to the television. Tim then called me on the phone and had the maintenance man get on the telephone and tell me that the television was disabled. Did I ask him to do this? No, but when he did I cried; my trust in him grew so much that day. Was he embarrassed to do this? I don't know, you would have to ask him, but I don't really think he cared what that man thought of him. Years later I am still telling people how much that one act of sacrifice impacted me.

Tim met with a therapist once a week, and occasionally we went to one together. He learned to "bounce his eyes" and look away if he thought that there was a questionable situation, and he avoided places where women would be dressed inappropriately, such as beaches, pools, health clubs, etc.

By far, the number one thing that Tim did that helped to restore my trust in him was to pray with me and lead use in a couple's devotion every morning. His prayer, without fail, asked God to help him bounce his eyes. By him doing this consistently, I have come to trust that God is right there with Tim, helping him to guard his heart and his mind.

Today Tim continues to work diligently for his healing. He is discovering new tools through the Pure Desire's *Seven Pillars of Freedom for Men* and he is also leading a Pure Desire group in our church.

Counselor's Corner

Tina mentions at the beginning of this chapter how the brain can be hijacked through sexual bondage. Dr. Ted Roberts is often asked, "Is sexual bondage a sin or an addiction?" His answer is "YES." It begins as a moral issue, but rapidly becomes a brain problem because a restructuring of the brain takes place.

Dr. Ted Roberts gives such a clear explanation of how sexually addictive behavior can change the structure of the brain that we are including this important information for you in this Counselor's Corner.

Dr. Roberts writes:[26]

I still remember the first time I read these jarring words of Paul. I thought, *That is me*!

> *I decide to do good, but I don't really do it; I decide*
> *not to do bad, but then I do it anyway.*
> Romans 7:19(MSG)

Those words so succinctly described the deepest frustrations of my life. I was totally committed to Christ, trying to serve him with all my heart yet I kept being drawn to porn or _____. (You can put your area of sexual struggle in the blank). "What is wrong with me?" I would cry. I thought that if I only tried harder the problem would go away. But that only made it worse because as I kept driving myself and shaming myself, the relapses only became more painful and crippling to my soul. The turning point came when I understood hell had hijacked my brain. Like Paul, I was literally a double-minded man at war with myself.

Your brain creates patterns and templates of action to help you deal more effectively with the demands of your day. Thus a man doesn't have to decide which hand to use to sign the check or which side of his face he will start shaving first in the morning. Your brain makes over three billion decisions per second, most of which are sub-conscious. In fact, it has been estimated that 90% of the decisions you make on a daily basis are sub-conscious in nature. You are on autopilot most of the time; this frees up your Prefrontal Cortex to develop and analyze new situations.

This isn't a problem until the autopilot is hijacked. We all have had the experience of finding ourselves in a room and we can't remember why we are there. Or we go into a room to do something and get distracted by something else that needs to be done. Like Paul, we were headed one place and ended up in another.

This is the common experience of someone struggling with sexual bondage. Sexual addiction is driven by the fact that you are dealing with a hijacked brain. That doesn't mean you can't help yourself; instead it means you are going to have to work hard at recalibrating and reprogramming your brain. You will have to purposely restructure the neurological connections of your brain that are setting you up. Otherwise you will continue to end up in the wrong place in life.

I was flying a long over-water flight in a fighter aircraft. The refueling range of such aircrafts is notoriously short; we therefore had to engage in several rendezvous with tanker aircraft. This is normally not a challenging endeavor but that day I had an autopilot that wouldn't easily disengage and it was pulling the plane off of the correct headings. The autopilot should have been my best friend. Long over-water flights can be very boring because you have to navigate by the instruments. There are no ground references to tell where you are so you are glued to the instrument panel; therefore, the autopilot can save you a lot of work. But in this case the autopilot was increasing my load by pulling the plane off course and refusing at times to disengage. I flew for hours battling with the thing, anxious that I might miss the tanker. The Pacific Ocean can be a very lonely place when you are frantically looking for the tanker as your fuel gauge rapidly drops to zero.

This illustration is a lucid picture of the mental battle the addict goes through because his faulty autopilot is trying to ignore the judgment or common sense of his input. When you are struggling with sexual bondage your Prefrontal Cortex commitment to Christ is usually being pulled off course by the autopilot of your Limbic System deep within your brain. When you continue to make choices that don't make any sense in your life, when you repeatedly make destructive sexual decisions, *it is a Limbic System problem.*

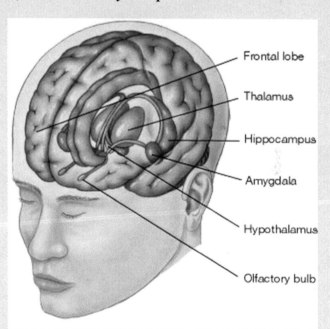

Your Limbic System is comprised of the amygdala, hippocampus, medial thalamus, nucleus accumbens, and basal forebrain, all of which connect to the anterior cingulate gyrus, which is the major gateway to the frontal cortex.[27] Don't let all those technical terms freak you out. We are going to look at just three parts of the Limbic System that drives addictive behavior.

1. The Hippocampus

This part of your inner brain consolidates learning by converting working memory into long-term memory and storing it in various regions of your brain. It is constantly comparing working memory with long-term memory, creating a sense of meaning in your thought process. For example, Alzheimer's progressively destroys neurons in the hippocampus, resulting in memory loss.

2. The Amygdala

This part of the brain works in association with the hippocampus. It is focused solely on survival. The amygdala is your early-warning system. It processes information even before the prefrontal cortex gets the message that something has happened. When you smile at the sight or sound of someone you love even before you consciously recognize her, the amygdala is at work. Recent research indicates that of all stimuli the brain (especially the male brain) processes, erotic scenes are processed 20% faster than anything else.[28] The amygdala defines what you see as being critical for your survival. It underlines in your memory what you should flee from or what you are willing to fight for so that you can survive. It also underlines what is so terrifying to you that you will just freeze, rendering you unable to respond to the threat. The amygdala also defines what food is critical for your survival and what is vital for you sexually.

An essential feature of brain anatomy is the fact that there are more connections running from the amygdala to the cortex than the other way around. This means the amygdala will win the battle every time. That is why Paul is in such despair in

Romans 7. When these two parts of your brain are at war with one another it is a bit like Mike Tyson facing off with Woody Allen. Fear, anger and sexual lusts which all stem from the amygdala are notoriously resistant to our ability to reason ourselves out of them. Once fearful reactions or traumatic memories (especially sexual ones) are burned into the amygdala, they tend to lock the mind and body into a recurring pattern of arousal. We have a great deal of difficulty restraining an excited amygdala.

Noted neuroscientist Joseph LeDoux, author of *The Emotional Brain* states that all strong emotional memories are neurobiologically indelible. I would agree with that statement apart from the power of the Holy Spirit. But if we allow the Holy Spirit's work to take place deep in our lives, our brains can be changed. Yet, I want to underline the fact that this process will not take place in a single prayer or Christian experience. It can only take place through the renewing of our minds. Much like a stroke victim, the addict has to re-grow various parts of his brain. He will have to renew his mind!

The first step is facing the pain. Initially the addict will be experiencing a greater level of pain, not less, because he has probably been medicating the emotional pain for years. Once he starts getting in touch with what has been going on deep within his thought processes the pain will rise to the surface. In his workbook he will be engaged in a lot of written responses. **This is not academic busy work!** Instead, this a process of getting his Prefrontal Cortex involved. Addicts tend to be very sharp; but when they are in a mental battle with their limbic system, it almost always wins the fight against their reasoning powers. The questions are not random. I have created them to help the brain focus. It is therefore important for your husband to do ALL THE EXERCISES because research has shown that the physical process of handwriting instead of typing on the computer engages more of the brain. It engages in a refining way much like adjusting the lens of a telescope can help you see the object clearly. The actual physical act of writing enhances mental change. **The addict will not get better unless he does the work necessary to renew his mind!**

3. The Nucleus Accumbens

The third element of your limbic system we will look at is your Nucleus Accumbens. In 2005, *Discovery* Magazine listed the discovery of the endogenous (which means internal) reward system as one of the greatest discoveries in the last 25 years of scientific research. The reason it is so significant is the fact that all drugs and addictive behaviors appear to involve the nucleus accumbens. Here is how the system works. The Nucleus Accumbens identifies a certain activity as one that needs to be repeated with the release of dopamine which floods across the synapses of the Prefrontal Cortex. This is where we get the "good feelings" from certain activities. But this reward system can be hijacked. For example, cocaine can flood the brain with a "super high" because it blocks the uptake pumps of the dopamine receptors in the brain. This results in a tidal wave of dopamine at the synapse creating an abnormal firing pattern in the neurons. **Over a period of time this literally rewires the brain.** Brain scans of cocaine addicts clearly show a reduced over-all brain function and specifically reduced Prefrontal Cortex activity. This is precisely why addicts can make dumb decisions; they simply can't think right.

Here is the connection with sexual addiction. Brain scans of sex addicts and gambling addicts show that the mere thought of sexual activity or gambling lights up their Nucleus Accumbens much like a cocaine addict. **Sexual addiction and gambling are "process addictions." The high is created by the action and not by a drug because the individual's own brain creates the drugs.**

This makes process addictions much more difficult to deal

with for two reasons.[29] First, the rationalization structures are harder to break through. That is why we immediately deal with breaking denial in the Seven Pillars for Men Workbook. If someone is abusing drugs and they have needle marks up and down their arms or their nose is being destroyed by snorting cocaine, it is harder for them to rationalize; the proof is right before them. A sex addict, however, can keep his activity hidden from view.

Secondly, process addictions have the capacity to create the immediate onset of a high like cocaine through things such as sexual fantasy. The battle with fantasy will lie at the core of ultimate victory and is also covered in the men's workbook.

Every time you act out or think about acting out, there is a surge of dopamine creating pleasure that triggers neurons and synapses in your brain. That sequence activates a set of beliefs (e.g. "I feel so overwhelmed or stressed, I will die without this fix") thus reinforcing limbic dysfunctional experiences that can go all the way back to early childhood. It just keeps reinforcing old destructive ways of coping with the pain in your life. Most of this takes place beyond the awareness of our conscious beliefs. This is exactly why Paul declared, "I want to do what is right (conscious beliefs), but I keep doing what is wrong (subconscious dysfunctional beliefs and patterns)." We keep repeating the old patterns of dancing with destruction.

This is precisely why just trying harder will not solve the problem because we are utilizing conscious processes to solve subconscious destructive processes. And more importantly this is why the ministry of the Holy Spirit is so important in our healing. He is the One who reveals Jesus to us (John 16). The Holy Spirit will uniquely reveal our subconscious processes that are entrapping us (Romans 8:11-17, 26-27).

All addictions are deadly traps, especially sexual addictions. Once you experience the dopamine spike of destructive sexual activity the brain tries to balance itself. Being a sexual addict means your limbic system is "on" most of the time through your sexual fantasies. Therefore the brain, in an attempt to balance things, reduces the production of dopamine that weakens the reward system. Now the trap has been sprung because you are compelled to act out, not to feel high but *just to feel normal*. This is why the sexual addiction has slowly been escalating over time. The addict has developed what is called "tolerance;" what has been used to sexually excite him doesn't turn him on now. That is why most sex addicts experience a decreased enjoyment in sexual relationships with their wife. Or the addict's other option is to pressure his wife to engage in sexual behavior he has observed in the pornography he has been viewing or the acting out he has experienced. The addict's pain and shame levels have only increased as he acted out because his commitment to Christ and moral incongruities are at odds with one another. His ability to medicate the pain through porn, masturbation, affairs or one night stands has continued to diminish. Welcome to insanity!

Research indicates that **as the addiction continues the brain is significantly changed.** Dr. Eric Nestler of the University of Texas has recently discovered that a hijacked dopamine cycle will produce a protein called Delta Fos B in the brain.[30] This protein will accumulate in the neurons, eventually throwing a genetic switch which causes changes that persist long after the reward cycle has stopped. This switch makes him overly sensitive to sexual stimuli. The addict is now far more prone to addiction because he experiences stronger cravings. His brain has become *sensitized* to the experience. Sensitization is different than tolerance. As tolerance develops, the addict needs more and more sexual acting out to get a pleasant effect.

But as sensitization develops the addict needs less and less of the experience for the cravings to increase. There are two separated systems in your brain: one for excitement and the other has to do with satisfying the pleasure cycle. Now he is caught in the vice of a vicious bondage. He is getting excited more and more easily but experiencing less and less fulfillment. Welcome to totally insanity!

(Diane Roberts) Because the brain has literally been hijacked in battle, the addict needs some incredibly powerful weapons to set him free. *The Seven Pillars of Freedom for Men's Workbook* is based on the latest research in neurochemistry. I have used these exercises time and again and have seen the deepest levels of bondage broken in men's lives. But you can have the finest clinical advice in the world and still be hopelessly in bondage. There are a number of things to which the addict must commit himself completely if he is ever going to get free.[31]

Dr. Roberts goes on to list the main commitments the husband needs to make: to honesty/transparency, to hard work, and to spiritual growth. Tina began to see all three of these things happening in Tim's life, and that gave her hope.

1. A commitment to honesty /transparency. Tina talked about the day Tim disclosed everything. That is huge for the wife, but at Pure Desire Ministries we have a few recommendation about disclosure. We recommend that disclosure *not* take place until the wife has the support of a counselor and/or small group. The men's small group leader can help prepare the husband as to how to share. The women's group leader can help the wife realize she will need to process his disclosure with the help of others. Pure Desire provides parameters on what should and shouldn't be shared concerning details and can prepare the wife through understanding what she needs to know in order to process the disclosure information.

2. A commitment to hard work. Tina shared how important

it was to her to see Tim doing **work** on his recovery, going to meetings and calling men. He also did counseling. Thirty percent of men in Pure Desire groups need to seek counseling besides being part of a group.

3. Spiritual Growth. Tim was praying and reading the Word of God daily. At Pure Desire we also recommend that the husband and wife pray together daily. Andy Stanley from Northpoint Community Church recently shared that the latest statistics have shown only eight percent of Christian couples pray together every night. Of those eight percent, only one in 10,000 couples divorce compared to the national average of one in two marriages end in divorce.

Notice that as Tim took these steps, he was moving out of isolation and building more in-depth relationships, not only with his wife, but also with other men. New relational experiences will change the addict's brain.

The other important step we emphasis in Pure Desire is dealing with the trauma that is driving the addiction. All of us have pain from our past and most of us are not even aware of the fact that it continues to drive our choices. As Dr. Roberts mentioned, the subconscious or limbic part of our brain drives our addictions. The limbic brain is totally developed by age six and our brain at that early age begins making decisions on what feels good and needs to be repeated, and what is painful and needs to be avoided.

Eighty to ninety percent of the men we deal with have a huge father wound that is driving the addiction. Their feelings of worthlessness started at an early age and are deeply hidden (and they are not in touch with), causing them to look for something to soothe the pain, such as porn or other sexual activity.

The hope communicated in this chapter is that with hard work, the help of other men, and honesty and transparency, the brain can change. God can do amazing things through the

Holy Spirit, just as He did in Tina and Tim's life.

❤ *Journal what stood out to you, the wife, as you read this chapter. What you can look for in your husband's behavior that will give you hope?*

❤ *If you are the husband, what impacted you most as you read this chapter? What are your next steps?*

| Peace Beyond the Tears

Chapter Eleven

Assessing the Damage:
Looking Inward & Working On Me

In my study of Scripture to write this book, I have learned much about God's love for me. I have learned that I am precious in His sight and He loves me (Isaiah 43:4). He knows my name and I am His (Isaiah 43:1). Think about that for a moment—God wants us! Precious...my daughters are precious to me. I would do anything for them and they are a part of me. God thinks of us that way! Additionally, God lavishes His love on us: "How great is the love the Father has lavished on us, that we should be called Children of God" (1 John 3:1).

He has told me in His Word that He will never leave me (Hebrews 13:5). So I know that no matter what happens between Tim and me, I will never be alone. God has told me that when I am afraid and I want to run away and hide from the world, He is there for me and is my hiding place (Psalm 32:7). He provides strength for my heart (Psalm 27:14).

When my youngest daughter was six years old, she would act very tough in front of people. When she got hurt (physically or emotionally) she would smile this pretend little smile and say, "I'm ok." I often watched her from a distance, wanting so bad to run over to her, scoop her up, and hug her. Instead I would catch her gaze and mouth, "Are you alright?" Sometimes she would just nod her little head, but other times she would slowly walk over to me, the tears welling up in her eyes with each step she took. When I hugged her and she buried her head in my chest (blocking out the rest of the world that she was trying so hard to be tough for), she would let down her guard and start to cry. As she shared her sorrow, I could feel her body soften as the weight of her pain left her. I held and comforted her until she felt like facing the world again. I cherished this time of comfort probably more than she did.

God is like that; He wants us to run into His arms so that He can comfort us. Instead, we pretend we are strong and don't need Him, and we turn to so many other things for comfort. Like my little daughter, we don't want the rest of the world to think that we are not strong or can't handle things on our own. If we will trust Him, run to Him, and bury our faces in His chest, telling Him of all our heartbreak and injury, He will comfort us. "Be merciful to me, O Lord, for I am in distress; my eyes grow weak with sorrow, my soul and my body with grief. My life is consumed by anguish and my years by groaning; my strength fails because of my affliction, and my bones grow weak.... But I trust in You, O Lord; I say, 'You are my God.' My times are in Your hands; deliver me from my enemies and from those who pursue me. Let your face shine on Your servant; save me in your unfailing love" (Psalm 31: 9-10, 14-16). Just like I watch my little girl from afar, waiting for her to come to me, God sees you; He is watching you, waiting for you to come to Him. "I will be glad and rejoice in your love, for you saw my affliction and knew the anguish of my soul" (Psalm 31:7).

He has taught me that even though Tim's addiction hurt me greatly, it is ultimately a battle between Tim and God, just as I have my own battles to face. Yes, I have a right to be angry and, yes, it is something that we need to deal with as a couple, but in the end, God and Tim need to face this together; in the end I must notice that I may be sinning by my reactions. No, I am not saying that my sinning in any way caused Tim to sin, and I am not saying that I should overlook Tim's sin. What I am saying is that God tells us exactly what we need to do to heal; asking for forgiveness of our own sin is one thing he tells us to do over and over again. "Then I acknowledged my sin to you and did not cover up my iniquity. I said, 'I will confess my transgressions to the Lord' –and you forgave the guilt of my sin" (Psalm 32:5).

Look at the story of Nehemiah who found out that the walls of Jerusalem were broken down and burned and that the people were in trouble. What did he do? First he cried and prayed for days (Nehemiah 1:4). Then he asked for forgiveness for himself and his family (Nehemiah 1:6-7). Next Nehemiah waited for God to respond to his prayers and to tell him what to do (Nehemiah 1:5-11). Nehemiah then made his needs known honestly, without covering anything up (Nehemiah 2:3-9). After his needs have been met, Nehemiah assessed the damage that has been done (Nehemiah 2:12-15), acknowledged the damage, faced it, and then asked for help (Nehemiah 2:17). He focused on God, not the problem (Nehemiah 2:18, 20).

Nehemiah trusted God (Nehemiah 2:20), came up with a plan, and then worked on that plan (Nehemiah 3). People began to mock Nehemiah and all the work that he was doing to rebuild the walls. Instead of listening to them and getting discouraged, Nehemiah prayed (Nehemiah 4:9). He set up protection and extra watch (prayer) in those areas that he might be weak (Nehemiah 4:13). Next, Nehemiah again realized he needed to refocus his thinking back to God and take care of himself as well as work on restoration (Nehemiah 4: 14, 16). He made a point to always be prepared for opposition, realizing that it would not be easy, but with God they would succeed (Nehemiah 4:17, 19-20).

Nehemiah got angry, stood up for what is right (Nehemiah 5:6), and continued to work at restoration even though it would have been so easy to give in, like all the other people that he saw around him (Nehemiah 5:16). Nehemiah did not let the enemy/opposition sidetrack him with their lies (Nehemiah 6: 3, 8). He asked God for help (Nehemiah 6:9), listened to God

(Nehemiah 7:5), and recognized and acknowledged the growth and healing that had taken place (Nehemiah 7:6-73. Then he praised God for all the work and healing that had been done (Nehemiah 8:6).

I love what happens next. Nehemiah, Ezra the priest, and the Levite instructors told the people not to mourn or weep because the day is holy to the Lord. Nehemiah added, "Do not grieve, for the joy of the LORD is your strength" (Nehemiah 8:10). I am amazed how much God wants to help us; He goes so far as to give us a step-by-step guide to healing and restoration! Reading the book of Nehemiah, I realized that healing takes time, faith, and perseverance—and God will help us to get through it.

The Tim that I now have plays with our girls, and he "sees" them. He listens to them talk with his whole heart, and he is tender toward them. He now takes an interest in my life and encourages me to experience life and to grow, even if it means he might have to pick up the slack in my absence or because of my busyness. He asks me in the mornings what he can do for me to make my day better; he calls me just to tell me that he loves me and he puts me above everything but God. He takes care of himself and runs almost every workday. He truly has become the spiritual leader of our home that I have always cried out for.

I will stop bragging on him, but I do so in order for you to see that God is faithful; He can do anything and change anybody, and He will take care of you. I wanted so badly to give up in the beginning. But I am so glad that I didn't. In the beginning it was a battle to just get out of bed; then it became a battle just to get through a day without crying. Slowly I began to live again, and now I wouldn't trade my life for anyone's. As I read through the Scriptures I see that God tells us that this is exactly what will happen for us, if we don't give up. Galatians 6:9 encourages us to be persistent in our pursuit of healthy living: "Let us not become weary in doing good, for at the proper time we will reap a harvest if we do not give up."

I am learning that once the pain is gone (or at least significantly softened) and I continue in my anger and resentment, I must deal with my own judgmental attitude. Not too long ago, we found ourselves at a neighborhood picnic celebrating the Fourth of July. We were having a wonderful time as a family until early afternoon when I noticed Tim getting edgy; eventually I noticed he was not with us anymore. When I looked around and saw some girls standing around in bikini bathing suits, I instantly got angry and started looking around for Tim. Within minutes my mind had him standing around with a group of men, watching girls. I found myself getting angrier and angrier, until my daughter handed me her cell phone and said, "Mom, Dad's at home." Tim told me he got tired of bouncing his eyes and trying to avoid the many distractions around him, so he had gone home and was watching the movie "Sister Act II" just to hear the praise music. At first I was relieved, but as the day wore on and I continued to celebrate with my kids, I found myself once again angry. I was tired and I wanted to be home; I became frustrated at the fact that Tim could just choose to step out and relax as I tried to make positive memories with our children. Later that evening I told Tim about my frustrations. I was surprised when he expressed that he wanted very badly to be with us and he felt sad to be left out of the celebration. God convicted me that night about how judgmental and selfish my attitude had become. He also pointed out how blessed I was to have a husband willing to forgo celebrations with his family to honor God and me. Tim loved me in the best way he knew how— and I got angry about it.

Sometimes I look at myself and become so overwhelmed by all the work that I see needs to be done in me. I want to see Tim the way Christ does and let go of any remaining bitterness and resentment. At the end of the day I look back on my reactions to the little annoyances throughout the day and my responses to them, and wonder if I will ever respond in a godly way. Will my first reaction always be negative? I hope not! I believe that one day I will be able to look on my day and know that I am living 1 Timothy 1:5: "The goal of this command is love which comes from a pure heart and a good conscience and a sincere faith."

I suggest that we pray for each other the words penned by the Apostle Paul to Jesus followers in the early church.

I pray that out of His glorious riches he may strengthen you with the power through the His Spirit in your inner being, so that Christ may dwell in your hearts through faith. And I pray that you, being rooted and established in love, may have power, together with all the saints, to grasp how wide and long and high and deep is the love of Christ, and to know this love that surpasses knowledge—that you may be filled to the measure of all the fullness of God.
Ephesians 3:16-19

Counselor's Corner

Tina's use of the scriptures in Nehemiah really do apply to every woman whose husband is struggling with sexual addiction. A few years ago a woman from one of my Betrayal & Beyond groups had just had some new disclosure. She found out her husband had had an affair with her best girlfriend fifteen years ago. He had been going through the healing process and had confessed everything else to her and the Holy Spirit convicted him about telling her everything. This was devastating to her, but I don't think it was by accident that Ted that very week was preaching on Nehemiah. He underlined the truth that for God to build a new foundation in our lives, He first has to clear all the rubble away. The couple shed many tears as they listened to the message; after the service, Ted and I prayed with them. Ted had used a square of concrete as part of his illustration for first clearing the rubble before you can lay a firm foundation. After we prayed over this couple's hurt and pain and released it to God, we had them stand on that square of concrete, declaring this truth over them: Now with all the rubble gone, God is able to build a powerful foundation built on honesty. That picture of them standing on a solid foundation will stay with them forever.

A pastor we counseled created another powerful picture of this principle. After being restored into ministry after moral failure, he planned a surprise recommitment of vows ceremony without letting his wife know ahead of time what would be happening. He had invited all those who stood with them through the rough healing process. As the wife entered, we were all holding umbrellas in front of us so she couldn't see who we were. As she approached the altar, we began lifting the umbrellas and surrounded them as a couple, holding our umbrellas over their heads as they recommitted themselves to each other. The husband said the Lord gave him the picture of the umbrellas that represented those who covered his wife and him during their healing journey, even though many others chose to attack and abandon them.

Like these couples, you may find it helpful to do something tangible to help seal the new healing taking place in you and your marriage.

❤ *Journal the Scripture in Nehemiah that stood out to you in relation to your current place in your healing process. As you journal, ask God to help you right where you are. Also ask him to reveal your next step.*

Chapter 12

What If He Doesn't Change?

*"But I will restore you to health and heal your
wounds," declares the Lord.*
Jeremiah 30:17

What if you followed the rules, prayed, and trusted God for complete restoration for your husband and your marriage but your husband still chooses not to change? What then? Does this mean that you didn't trust enough or do things right? No, not at all. Our husbands are human, and if they are caught in this web of addiction they are also incredibly wounded. It is up to them to change their behaviors and stop the addictive cycle, not you.

We can only do our part in the healing; we cannot take on our husband's recovery as well. If we do that, we risk becoming co-dependent. In *Co-Dependent No More,* Melody Beattie describes a codependent person as "one who has let another person's behavior affect him or her, and who is obsessed with controlling that person's behavior."[32]

Someone who is codependent tends to overlook behaviors and make excuses for the one who is hurting them. She tends to fault herself for her own problems and for her family's problems. She avoids conflicts, discounts her own feelings and perceptions, and tries to appear cheerful and to give the impression that things do not hurt as badly as they really do. Codependents become stuck in their healing; emotions are buried inside, but they will surface. Depression and passive aggressive behavior, as well as over reacting to situations, can result. That is why God tells us to carry our own burdens and let others carry theirs, as Paul writes in Galatians. "Each one should test his own actions. Then he can take pride in himself, without comparing himself to somebody else, for each one should carry his own load" (Galatians 6: 4-5).

In looking back, I see many ways in which I was becoming co-dependent. I worried so much that Tim would act out again that I became obsessed with where his eyes looked or how long it had been since we last had sex. I was constantly apologizing to keep the peace, even if I was not at fault. I paid close attention to Tim's emotions and if he seemed unhappy or edgy at all, I would go out of my way to try and remove whatever I thought was causing his stress. If he was happy then the entire family was happy; if he was unhappy we were all stressed. If you can identify with some of these statements, I encourage you to learn more about co-dependency. My girls learned to cope in co-dependent ways as well by watching me.

What can you do if you don't see change? You love him so much and you want to stay married to him, but you don't want to live the way you have been living any longer. He says he has changed, but then he relapses. What now? Ladies, I praise God that I have not had to deal with this. But the reality is that there is a possibility that Tim may relapse. What then? Do I leave him? Do I simply forgive him? Do I start all over in this mess called recovery?

I don't know what I'd do, but from what I know to be true, I know I WOULD NOT BE ALONE. God would be my constant companion and I would surround myself with godly people to speak truth into my life. I would urge Tim to attend Every Man's Battle or connect with a Pure Desire group. I would urge him to get counseling again. I would guard my heart and establish strong boundaries to protect my children and myself from any more pain. And if he still chose to act out,

I would no longer want to be married to him. But this is just what I think I would do. We never know what we are going to do until the time comes. I will say this though; we all have different levels of tolerance. I pray that if the time ever does come when Tim returns to his addiction, that I am so grounded in the love of God that nothing will shake me. I pray that I see myself as God's little girl and I see my complete worth in Him and not in what Tim does or doesn't do.

If your husband continues to act out I am so sorry for your pain. Please do these things:

- Surround yourself with people who can show you the love of Christ. Do not face this alone.
- Seek wise counsel from church leaders and friends you can trust.
- Know that it is not your fault and that you do not need to stay in a toxic relationship.
- Know that your Father in heaven loves you so powerfully. Ground your identity in Jesus. Study God's Word and find out who God says you are rather than defining yourself by your husband's behavior.
- Journal your thoughts, emotions, and dreams.
- Tell your story. It helps to talk. You do not need to protect your husband. You need to take care of you and your family. Find your voice with safe people who can support you.
- Set healthy boundaries and be accountable to other women to follow these boundaries.
- Don't pretend you're OK. Cry out to Jesus and ask Him to help you. Ask Him to bind up your wounds and set you free from all the lies that you have been told over the years. Ask Him to help you to see the reality of what is and the reality of who you are. And then ask Him to help you to accept that reality and move and grow forward.
- Find ways to pamper and take care of you. As you have

walked through the ups and downs of your relationship, you have probably focused all your energy on his behavior and health. To walk in health and be able to care for your children or others around you, you need to take care of you.

Knowing the stages of grief/loss will help prepare you for what to expect along the way. The titles of the stages are adapted from the work of Michael Dye in his Genesis Process[33] workbooks. I have shared my own comments and experiences under each stage.

First Stage: Shock and Denial. In this phase I found myself going into survival mode. I tried to stay busy to avoid the pain and then became exhausted trying to do life's daily tasks. I obsessed over my eating and exercise, and some days found it almost physically impossible to get out of bed. I felt confused and humiliated. I remember telling myself that I was making a big deal out of nothing. One time I went for a walk, hoping to be hit by a car, thinking that everyone's life would be better without me and my pain. I felt stupid, deceived, and extremely alone. It would have been wonderful to have had women to talk to at this time, but my journaling helped me immensely.

Second Stage: Anger and Fear. I hated Tim with such passion, but was afraid that he would leave me. I was angry at God, angry at other women, and I was even angry at my own daughters because they were young and beautiful. I remember thinking that after all of the abuse I felt I had lived through in my past, I deserved to feel loved. I remember thinking that God must hate me to allow this to happen. I felt powerless, stupid, and afraid. And I felt extremely guilty for feeling any of it at all.

Third Stage: Bargaining. This is where I found myself fasting and trying to manipulate God. I bargained with God, promising that if He would keep Tim from ever going back to the porn, I would be the perfect wife, mother, and Christian. I felt completely helpless and vulnerable, thinking that if I just pleaded enough or was good enough then Tim would change. I finally had to realize that I was powerless to change Tim. All I could do was set healthy boundaries, follow through with them, and realize that no matter what happened in my marriage, I would be ok.

Fourth Stage: Sadness/Depression. Some days I was so overwhelmed with sadness that I felt like I couldn't breathe. One day I was walking through Target with my daughters; my knees almost buckled beneath me when I saw the images of young girls in their bathing suits on wall posters. I realized there was no way to get away from the pain of betrayal. I felt completely abandoned and worthless. My days were a blur and I remember wanting to melt into a puddle and disappear, but also wanting so desperately to be my old, happy self again. I no longer trusted myself and my feelings. I also had to grieve my loss of innocence. I could no longer look at old family photos without pain. I grieved the loss of the life that I thought I had, as well as the life that I thought I was going to have in the future.

Fifth Stage: Acceptance & Repair. This is when I found my "new normal." I began to rebuild the relationship with my husband. I started to find a balance in life again with family and routines. I found myself enjoying things that I used to enjoy, as well as finding new hobbies and interests. This stage can occur anywhere between year one and year three, and even into year four.

Sixth Stage: Growth and Family. I learned how to resolve conflicts, and restore intimacy and healthy sexuality. Tim and I began to relate as a couple, apart from the addiction. This is a wonderful place to be. We are not healed completely, but we are learning to relate in a new way. We are learning to trust each other, and to value each other's opinion, even if it is different from our own. And we are learning to enjoy each other again, as friends and as lovers.

I don't know where you are in your healing. I don't know what your past or your future look like. All I know is that we have a God who loves us beyond measure. He will hold you and carry you through this trial and on into the next. His grace *is* enough. His power *is* enough. He *will* see you through. You need to hold on. He *will* rescue you from the battleground that has left you broken and bleeding. When you can't or don't trust, you can simply pray, "Lord, I believe; help me with my unbelief!"

In one year, two years, maybe four years, I am believing that you and your husband can both look back on what you have experienced and see God's touch on your life all along the way—and see Him weeping over your tears, cheering you on, and turning your mourning into dancing.

God bless you, my sister and friend.

Counselor's Corner

- ❤ *Journal some ways you might be able to identify with Tina and how she found herself slipping into codependent behavior, trying to control her spouse or the circumstances to avoid pain.*

- ❤ *Journal where you are in the grief stages and how you can relate to what Tina has shared.*

Tina pointed out the crazy dance of codependency that results if we start trying to carry our husband's load. *Betrayal & Beyond* describes the impact of codependency:

> The codependent woman is desperate to stop her husband from acting out and yet her help doesn't help him; it hurts him by allowing him to be more entrenched in addictive paths through shame, isolation and secrecy. By attempting to fix the problem, the codependent woman interferes with the natural consequences of the addiction. Moreover, she continues to put herself in a place where she cannot get the help she needs. Rescuers operate with a sense of shame hoping beyond hope that things will turn around if they can just solve the problem. They do not know how to set healthy boundaries and continually fail to define who they are, instead morphing into whatever shape that is required to keep the addict from acting out.[34]

Practicing healthy self-care and setting healthy boundaries can help you avoid codependency. We have mentioned having a Safety Plan that helps you begin to establish those healthy boundaries.

When working on a Safety Plan, think through what you need to see your husband doing in order to begin to trust. Then decide the natural consequences of any relapse, and how you will follow through with those consequences. One gal I counseled required he be out of the home for a week if he used porn and acted out, but when the time came they had no finances for that to happen. I gave her some creative ideas: he can stay with someone in his group or sleep in the car in the garage. Or, if it is warm enough, he can set up a tent in the back yard, come in for showers, and take his food outside or be with the family only for mealtime.

Another gal decided she needed him to get a phone with no internet or texting available because his phone internet use caused him to act out. Another woman required that all computer use would occur in the kitchen or family room where everyone congregated. Also, she was the only one who had the password.

If there is infidelity and you are still willing to work on the marriage, you may need to work with a counselor and/or pastor by yourself for a while. If you separate, you may want to require him to be in counseling or be part or a men's sexual addiction group before he is allowed to live with you again. He must also be willing to do whatever it takes to restore the marriage. It will require a lot of hard work and he will have to commit to that.

These natural consequences are not meant to be punitive, but rather to help you to find your voice and also help him to see that the pain on the outside (sleeping elsewhere) will be greater than the pain and trauma on the inside that he has been medicating. This is how God deals with us. He says if we walk with Him in His ways we will experience blessing; if we choose to walk in our ways, separate from Him, we will experience curses. Your husband has choices, just as you do.

Many of our Pure Desire men's leaders have reported that they see the most sobriety growth in men whose wives have a safety plan with natural consequences. These men begin to take the process more seriously because they know there will be natural consequences if they relapse.

Decide ahead of time what you are willing to do and then ask your support group of women to hold you accountable to follow through.

Epilogue

Remember the story I shared at the beginning of this book? I wrote in my journal about myself as a doll, created to be bought by one man who would have complete control over my life and happiness.

God has taught me so much through seven years of recovery. I am not an object! I am fearfully and wonderfully made (Psalm 139:14); I am a child of God (John 1:12); God calls me by name and says I am His (Isaiah 43:1). I hope you, too, are able to see that you are not an object and that God loves you beyond measure, right now, just the way you are, where you are. Unlike the doll in the story, there will never be a time when you or I are "not quite right." God "knit me together in my mother's womb" (Psalm 139:13), and He reminds me that I am precious and honored in His sight and He loves me (Isaiah 43:4).

I hope you also have come to realize that God made you for a purpose apart from your husband and that your happiness is not dependent on him. I pray that you understand your husband's addiction has nothing to do with you, what you look like, or what you did and did not do.

In the doll story, the doll maker assures Tina that one day she would be wanted. Friend, this is so non-biblical! God's Word says that before we are born, He knew us, loved us, and wanted us. We are chosen (Ephesians 1:4) and adopted into God's family (Ephesians 1:5). Unlike the doll, we are cherished because of who we are right now. I have come to realize that there was nothing that I could have done to make Tim want me more. God calls me to seek after Him and His desires for my life, not my husband's (Matthew 6:33).

The doll waits to be rescued. You and I are not dolls; we are not helpless, nor designed to live in unhealthy dependence on others. I am to work on myself and my relationship with Christ, and be the best "me" I can be.

God *has* turned my mourning into dancing.

New Life's Women In the Battle workshop and Pure Desire's Betrayal & Beyond groups are places women can get the support that I so desperately needed in the beginning. As I watch women walk through this healing journey with the support of other women, I am amazed at how different it is to heal in community instead of alone like I did. As I share my story with others and help them navigate through their own stories, I continue to find healing from my own past. I am realizing the value and impact of having other women around me, and the necessity of allowing myself time and grace to heal.

Recently I was able to visit with a darling lady from Australia at a New Life workshop. She told me that the one thing she missed the most since she found out about her husband's addiction was laughing with God. I didn't know what she meant by this until I was driving to an Every Man's Battle workshop where Tim and I were scheduled to speak briefly to the men attending the event. I was thinking about my life, how far Tim and I had come, and that he is a great husband. *I would go through all that we had gone through these past six years all over again,* I thought, *to have the life I now have.* As I was thinking about how much I loved my husband, I suddenly began to cry. I began to thank God for where we were in life when my tears turned into laughter. For the first time in my life, I knew what it meant to laugh with God. The peace and joy that I felt at that moment were incredible beyond words.

The Canyon Revisited

Remember the Grand Canyon trip I planned? I live in Dallas, Texas, which is extremely flat, and I was training to hike a huge, deep canyon—no small feat for a flat-lander. I spent quite a bit of money preparing, as well as participated in fundraising for the charity for which I was hiking. The weekend our group was scheduled to hike the Grand Canyon was the same weekend that our US Government decided to shut down all national parks until further notice! I felt let down by God and extremely disappointed as we boarded our plane a few days later, having no idea what God had in store for us.

Our group of forty soon discovered that an edge of the Canyon is under the control of the Havasupai Indian Reservation and not under the jurisdiction of the National Park Service. These trails are not maintained to the same standard as the more highly visited tourist areas of the Grand Canyon. No park rangers patrol to keep visitors safe, bathroom stops are few, and water is only available at the bottom rather than every few miles. But at the bottom of the hike (ten miles in) we were guaranteed an incredible view of Havasu Falls. As excited as I was, the rules had now changed and this was not what I expected. I had told everyone that I was going to hike the Grand Canyon. Did this count?

The next morning before the sun rose, we boarded a bus headed to the entrance of our adventure. We were told to write our names on the back of one leg calf and how we hoped to experience God on the other. "I AM" I Wrote on my calf. I wanted God to show me that it was all Him and none of me.

Part sandy, part rocky trail was not at all what we had trained for. Within a few hours one of my legs and one of my knees began to hurt. Not muscle hurt, but injury hurt. I ignored the pain and didn't say anything to my hiking buddy. About a third of the way down, I knew something was wrong, as every step brought tears to my eyes. *If only I can make it to the bottom the terrain will change and I will be fine*, I reasoned.

My hiking buddy noticed me trying desperately not to bend my knee and she asked me if I was OK. I told her I was fine, but she offered to tape up my knee anyway. I told her I didn't want it taped because I didn't want anyone to treat me differently or see me as weak. (Sound familiar?) The pain continued to increase and I continued to try to ignore it. I did, however, start to pray and ask God to take away the pain and to not let anyone see. I did my best to take in the natural beauty all around, but I found myself looking down at the ground instead of around me, all the while trying to hide my pain from everyone.

Through the dust and the dirt that I couldn't see beyond as I hiked, past the mountains and rocks, was hidden something breathtaking and life-giving. At the bottom of the canyon, I felt small and yet so loved as I viewed a spectacular, immense, and powerful waterfall. As I looked around, I sensed that God was with me, holding me. The mist refreshed and motivated me— and it was here all the time, even before I had seen it.

We rested and lingered in the beauty of the falls. Since I was sure my pain would not return on the journey back up the canyon, I stepped out with renewed energy and resolve. Quickly I realized hiking up hurt even worse than hiking down, and every step brought pain. It was getting more difficult to pretend that everything was fine. I was afraid that if anyone found out, they would make me stop or see me as weak. I made sure my buddy and I were near the front of the pack, thinking that if I stayed with the fast hikers no one would suspect anything.

When we stopped for water at a little village a few miles up the trail, one of the leaders questioned me, gave me medicine as well as encouragement, and prayed with me. I realized I had been relying on my own strength and had not been asking God to show up. God showed me that the hike down had been hard, especially since I did not ask for help. He impressed on me that I was not judged because of my pain, and that the words "I AM" on the back of my calf were not simply words.

As we continued to hike up, our feet were in pain from blisters; we were hot, tired, and dirty, and I wondered if I could make it to the top. About five hours from the end of the hike I saw a large mountain looming in the distance. I whispered to my hiking buddy, asking if it was the one big mountain that we had to hike at the end. In my question, I was asking, "Is it almost over?" I was in so much pain I did not think I was going to make it. I needed to see the finish line, to know there was an end. That was not our final mountain. Had I have known how far we yet had to go, I think I would have panicked. I found myself reading the words written on the calves of people ahead of me, including my friend and hiking buddy who had written the word "SURRENDER." "Surrender, Tina, this is not about you," I heard God whisper again and again.

That last mountain was HARD. At one point I lost my footing and stumbled to the side, precariously close to the edge. My friend had seen and asked me if I was ok. She knew how close I was, she knew how much pain that I was in, but she didn't ask me if I wanted to stop; she kept going, knowing that if I stopped I might rest in my pain and not continue. And there was nothing to do but continue up. Stopping was not an option.

Finally, from a distance we heard long-awaited voices cheering us on, "YOU CAN DO IT!!!" From far away they were so small, but their encouragement gave us new strength. We could see the end! I thought this part would be easy since we were almost there, but the pain, exhaustion, and utter overwhelming-ness of it all was catching up to me, and I almost couldn't breathe. By the time I saw their faces I was ready to give up. When I told my friend I didn't think that I could go on, she smiled and encouraged me forward. Then I saw her face and realized I was not alone; she was tired, sore, and overwhelmed, too. We had been in this together from the beginning—training, disappointment, and uncertainty. And we were going to finish it together. I forcibly lifted my legs one step at a time and willed myself forward, calling on Jesus as I silently sang praises to Him. Overwhelmed, elated, humbled, and broken we were greeted at the finish by a wonderful team of friends who offered us food and drinks and lovingly washed our feet. My dear, sweet hiking buddy hugged me and we cried on each other's shoulders, "We made it! We made it! We made it!"

We sat at the top of the canyon for hours, enjoying dinner prepared by volunteers, sharing stories of our journeys to the top, and taking in the beauty surrounding us. As I sat there, I thought of you, dear reader, and of our journeys through recovery. I thought about how we planned for our lives to go a certain way, we had so many wonderful expectations, much like my plans for the Grand Canyon. How unexpectedly and suddenly plans changed and how the very idea behind the change was incomprehensible, much like our government shutdown. I thought about how we walk into the unknown, having no idea what the next day will bring, and how much our hearts and minds determine our reactions. Then I thought about how we may think that we are relying on God, but often we are relying on our own strength. How we are afraid to be vulnerable and let others see our pain for fear they will judge us or find us weak or lacking. How, when we reach out to other safe people, we realize we are not alone and how that realization makes it so much easier to cope and go on.

I thought about how if we were able to see the path ahead of us in its entirety, we would probably be so overwhelmed we would give up. But God doesn't let us see the whole plan. He asks us to trust Him one step at a time. I also thought about how we often become overwhelmed and feel like we can't breathe, and it is then that we need to start singing praises to our God who loves us so much.

I thought about seeing the pain and exhaustion in the eyes of my sweet hiking buddy. I had assumed she was breezing through the hike and that I was weak. I realized that no matter how things may seem, how strong others may appear, if we look around us, we would realize others are hurting. Like us, they may be afraid to show the pain for fear of being weak or vulnerable.

God showed me that day that He truly is all I need and He is with me every step of the way. He will whisper encouragement in our ears and He will show us others who are hurting and allow us to heal together. And best of all, He celebrates each and every victory with us along the way.

Tina at Havasu Falls, the bottom of the Grand Canyon, Arizona

Resources

| Peace Beyond the Tears

Signs of Addiction:
You Are Not Crazy

Some or all of these may be indicators that your husband is in the midst of a sexual addiction. He may:

- Become good at telling "white lies." If they answer your questions at all, the responses seem vague or evasive. You may find evidence of hiding, lying, and secretive behavior.

- Respond defensively, especially when asked about the source of his addiction. If you question the amount of time spent on the computer, or why he came to bed so late, he may get angry or become uncharacteristically edgy.

- Start to seem different. He sometimes acts irrational. Feeling a sense of worthlessness, like there is something wrong with him because he has been acting out, he may pick fights or blame others for his bad attitude. He may make excessive demands on you or your children in order to justify his use of porn. When Tim was on the computer he would yell at the kids if they were the least bit disruptive.

- Spend large amounts of time on the computer, and may demand privacy or may start to stay up later. He may start to complain of back/neck aches or wrist problems. Tim constantly had a "project" going on that required him on the computer. I would put the girls to bed and come down an hour later and he would still be there. He would tell me he would be right up and to go to bed without him. When he finally did come up he would either take a shower or climb into bed with his back to me. Regardless of the mood he was in when I left him downstairs he was almost always angry by the time he came to bed.

- Complain that his wrist or hands hurt. Tim would hold them out to me to rub anytime I got close to him. He used to say that he had carpal tunnel syndrome.

- Express concern with your appearance. He may ask you to dress differently or loose/gain weight. Tim bought me lingerie while away on travel and yet never wanted to see me in them. He requested that I shave my pubic area "just for fun." I have come to know that most porn actresses/model are bare.

- Change his sexual habits, either becoming disinterested or excessively interested. He may want to try new things or may become rough during sex. He may have a more difficult time becoming aroused or he may need more and more stimulation to have an orgasm.

- Become less social. As he lives in this fantasy world of porn, it becomes more difficult to relate in the real world.

- Seem emotionally distant during sex. This is the sign I noticed the most. After we had sex I would feel used, empty, and rejected. He would turn over with his back to me and fall asleep without a word.

Counselor's Corner

Tina points out many symptoms of someone caught up in sexual bondage. Many sex addicts have an intimacy and attachment disorder and, because at an early age they learned to use porn to medicate their pain, they have a hard time relating to a real woman. A great resource for understanding sexual anorexia can be found on Douglas Weiss's website, intimacyanorexia.com.

What a Polygraph Test Can & Cannot Do[35]

The polygraph test is one tool that can be used to begin to restore trust in a relationship. It can be given within 30 days of disclosure and can be followed up every 90 days by another one to ensure greater accountability. If trust begins to grow, you may want to repeat the test every six months, and then go to one every year, depending on the type of addiction.

Most sex addicts don't like the idea of a polygraph test because they have never had their behavior measured objectively. But over time, we have found that men who are serious about walking in health actually see this as a helpful measure of how they are moving towards health. Also, when they know there will be a follow-up test, it helps them to think twice about the temptation to fall back into old patterns.

The polygraph cannot guarantee that he will not lie again or that he will stop his addictive behavior, but it can promote safety and trust. Although this tool can begin to help reestablish trust, the goal is to eventually leave the tool behind and begin to trust based on a growing intimacy in the relationship.

Caution! for wives who have requested this test:

- Be careful that the polygraph not be used to feed into the codependent need to be a detective.
- If the husband passes, don't challenge the test. If you have concerns, wait until the next polygraph test. If there are inconsistencies in his behavior, expect them to be revealed in the next polygraph test.

Full disclosure polygraph. The most effective polygraph tests are "full disclosure polygraphs" that take between two to three hours initially. A full disclosure will collect the addict's sexual history and then the examiner will ask any specific questions requested by you. If you are working with a Pure Desire Counselor, he will help your spouse write out that full history ahead of time. The spouse then takes that history with him to the polygrapher, along with about five yes or no questions from the wife.

You can check the yellow pages under "polygraph" or do an internet search for "polygraph examiner." Or check with local attorneys who can put you in contact with someone qualified to administer a full disclosure polygraph.

What do I do with the results? It is best to have the results sent to a counselor who can debrief you as a couple.

Questions for the polygraph test. See *Betrayal & Beyond Book 1* (pages 143-144) for some questions the wife may want included in the polygraph test.

Personal Safety Action Plan[36]

The following is a shortened version of three steps from the Safety Plan in Betrayal & Beyond Book 2.

Step one helps you to think through those things you need to be doing for your own personal health and growth.

Step two helps you decide what you need to see your spouse doing in order to begin to regain trust.

Step three helps you think through the natural consequences of what will happen if your spouse relapses.

Although you do not have control over your spouse's addiction and healing, you do have a choice about how to respond to him, what you want your own healing to look like, and how to provide protection for yourself and your children.

Remember, every woman's situation is unique when facing the issues surrounding betrayal. **Choose the steps and strategies that are most appropriate and helpful to your life and situation.** Not every option presented will be applicable to you. Before implementing anything in your Safety Action Plan, please seek pastoral input from someone who understands addiction.

Step 1: Actions for My Own Healing

I need to focus my energy on my own restoration. I can use some or all of the following strategies:

____ A. Attend a women's small group that understands addiction and healing.

____ B. Commit to the process of identifying and healing root issues in my life (e.g., trauma, codependency, anger, addictions, helplessness.)

____ C. Commit to daily prayer and Scripture reading.

____ D. Begin/continue classes or counseling for healing of childhood wounds.

___ E. Commit to sharing with an accountability partner what I've studied and applied, as well as insights gained throughout the week.

___ F. Seek counseling for current personal, sexual addiction, and/or marriage issues if needed.

___ G. Commit to reading healing-oriented literature about shame issues, boundaries, codependency, trauma, etc.

___ H. Commit to personal journaling.

___ I. Arrange for STD testing if infidelity has occurred.

___ J. For my own spiritual growth, I will make a commitment to a local church.

___ K. I can also _____.

Step 2: Actions for My Partner's Healing.

My spouse is responsible for his own healing. I need to see him using some or all of the following strategies in order for me to begin trusting him again:

___ A. Attend a men's small healing group that utilizes the Pure Desire *Seven Pillar of Freedom Men's Workbook.*

___ B. Be committed to the process of sexual purity.

___ C. Commit to daily prayer and Scripture reading.

___ D. Commit to accountability with a small group and /or accountability partner regarding his sexual purity.

___ E. Be open to sharing with me what he has studied and applied, as well as insights gained throughout the week.

___ F. Commit to reading healing-oriented literature about shame issues, boundaries, codependency, trauma, etc.

___ G. Begin/continue with any classes dealing with wounds and shame from the past.

___ H. Arrange for STD testing if infidelity has occurred.

___ I. Polygraph test (see Resource section in this book for more information).

___ J. Seek personal counseling if needed.

___ K. Attend church regularly for spiritual growth and support.

___ L. Covenant Eye's put on all computers for computer screening and reporting. (Contact www.covenanteyes.com for more information.)

___ M. He can also _____.

Step 3: Action During a Sexual Addiction Relapse.

My partner may relapse. When this is disclosed to me, I may use a variety of strategies in order to protect my children and myself without falling back into codependent behavior. I can use some or all of the following strategies, and the consequences may double if he does not share with me and his group within 24-48 hours of the relapse:

___ A. I will ask my spouse to sleep in another room for _____ weeks/months until sexual purity has been obtained.

___ B. I will ask my spouse to move out for _____ weeks/months until sexual purity has been re-established.

___ C. I can call _____ for counseling and/or prayer support.

___ D. I will ask my spouse to call and make an appointment with his counselor, pastor, or healing group leader for advice and accountability.

___ E. If I choose to leave my home, I will go to _____. If I cannot go to the location above, then I can go to _____. (Decide this even if you don't think there will be a next time.)

___ F. I will ask my spouse to stop internet use for_____ days or totally abstain.

___ G. If infidelity has occurred with someone in his workplace, I will ask that he transfer to a different department or location or find a new job within _____ days.

___ H. I will ask my spouse to have no further contact with a person with whom he has been sexual or inappropriate.

___ I. I will call his parole officer to inform him of any parole violations.

___ J. I can also _____.

Further steps are recommended in *Betrayal & Beyond Book 2* if you need to protect yourself and/or your children from violence or abuse. There are also suggestions for support during a separation.

For Further Reading

Recommended by Tina Harris

- *The Secrets Women Keep* by Dr. Jill Hubbard
- *Sacred Marriage* by Gary Thomas
- *Reframe Your Life* by Stephen Arterburn
- *The Wounded Woman* by Steve Stephens and Pam Vredevelt
- *When You Love Too Much* by Stephen Arterburn
- *Co-Dependant No More* by Melody Beattie

Recommended by Diane Roberts

- *Pure Desire* by Dr. Ted Roberts (a chapter for women is included)
- *Betrayal & Beyond Books 1, 2 and 3* by Diane Roberts, Pure Desire Ministries International
- *Intimacy Anorexia* by Douglas Weiss, PH.D
- *Mending a Shattered Heart: A Guide for Partners of Sex Addicts* by Stephanie Carnes
- *Boundaries* by Dr. Henry Cloud and Dr. John Townsend
- *An Affair of the Mind* by Laurie Hall
- *Restoring the Pleasure* by Clifford L. Penner & Joyce J. Penner
- *Your Sexually Addicted Spouse* by Barbara Steffens, and Marsha Means
- Additional resources for men & women at puredesire.org

Endnotes

[1] Patrick Carnes, *Don't Call It Love* (New York: Bantam Books, 1991) 14.

[2] Steven Arterburn, *Every Man's Battle* (Colorado Springs, CO: Waterbrook Press, 2009)

[3] Dr. Ted & Diane Roberts, *Sexy Christians* (Grand Rapids, MI: Baker Books, 2011) 226

[4] Steven Arterburn, *When You Love Too Much* (Ventura, CA: 2004) 83.

[5] Ibid. 91.

[6] Ibid, 99.

[7] Ibid, Addictive Cycle, main points summarized from Chapter 4.

[8] Ibid, Chapter 4.

[9] Ibid. Chapter 4.

[10] Pure Desire Ministries International. puredesire.org.

[11] Craig Gross, *Porn Stats*. XXX Church (June 04, 2010).

[12] Steven Arterburn, *When You Love Too Much* (Ventura, CA: 2004) 96.

[13] Ted Roberts, *Pure Desire* (Ventura, CA: Regal, 2008) 287.

[14] Patrick Carnes, ed., *Clinical Management of Sex Addiction* (New York: Brunner-Routledge, 2002) 14-18.

[15] Ted Roberts, *Seven Pillars of Freedom Workbook for Men* (Gresham, OR: Pure Desire Ministries International, 2009) 272-273, written by Diane Roberts.

[16] Steven Arterburn, *When You Love Too Much* (Ventura, CA: 2004) 165.

[17] Dr. Omar Minwalla, Licensed Psychologist and Clinical Sexologist. http://understandinghersideofthestory.com/ The Sexual Trauma Model.html, 2008.

[18] Deborah Corley & Jennifer Schneider, *Disclosing Secrets* (Wickenburg, AZ: Gentle Path Press, 2002) 141.

[19] Dr. James Dobson, http://www.focusonthefamily.ca/marriage/divorce-separation/hope-for-couples-in-crisis

[20] Linda J. MacDonald, M.S., LMFT, *How to Help Your Spouse Heal From Your Affair* (Gig Harbor, WA: 2010) 28-30 (short summary of main points). For purchase see website: www.lindajmacdonald.com.

[21] Deborah Corley & Jennifer Schneider, *Disclosing Secrets* (Wickenburg, AZ:

Gentle Path Press, 2002) 141.

[22] Diane Roberts, *Betrayal & Beyond Book 1* (Gresham, OR: Pure Desire Ministries International, 2009) 93.

[23] L.B. Smedes, *Forgive and Forget: Healing The Hurts We Don't Deserve* (New York: Pocket Books, 1984) 38.

[24] Diane Roberts, *Betrayal & Beyond Book 3*, (Gresham, OR: Pure Desire Ministries International, 2010) 16-17.

[25] Diane Roberts, *Betrayal & Beyond Book 3* (Gresham, OR: Pure Desire Ministries International, 2010) 127.

[26] Dr. Ted Roberts. *Pure Desire Seven Pillars of Freedom Men's Workbook*, adapted from Introduction-3 (Gresham, OR: Pure Desire Ministries International, 2009) 31-34.

[27] John Ratey, *A User's Guide to the Brain* (New York: Vintage Books: 2001) 227.

[28] Patrick Carnes, *The 40-Day Focus: Book One* (Carefree, AZ: Gentle Path Press, 2005) 20.

[29] *Process Addictions: Approaches for Professionals"* notes from seminar presented by Foundations Recovery Network, April 22-24, 2009.

[30] Eric Nestler, *"Psychogenomics: Opportunities for understanding addictions."* Journal of Neuroscience, (2001) (21) 8324-8327.

[31] Ted Roberts. *Pure Desire Seven Pillars of Freedom Men's Workbook*, adapted from Introduction-3 (Gresham, Oregon: Pure Desire Ministries International: 2009) 33-34.

[32] Melody Beattie, *Co-Dependent No More: How to Stop Controlling Others and Start Caring for Yourself.* www.hazeldon.org/bookstore.. 31.

[33] Michael Dye and Patricia Fancher, *The Genesis Process: A Relapse Prevention Workbook for Addictive/Compulsive Behaviors* (Auburn, California: Michael Dye, 1998; 3rd Edition 2007) 115. www.genesisprocess.org.

[34] Diane Roberts, *Betrayal & Beyond Book 2* (Gresham, OR: Pure Desire Ministries International, 2010) 70-71. Used with permission.

[35] Diane Roberts, *Betrayal & Beyond Book 1* (Gresham, OR: Pure Desire Ministries International, 2009) 143-144. Used with permission

[36] Diane Roberts, *Betrayal & Beyond Book 2* (Gresham, OR: Pure Desire Ministries International, 2010) 141-143. Used with permission.